Vamp 'Til Ready

Al Lerner

*Sandra & Tony
Thanks for being
her with us*

Al Lerner

Vamp 'Til Ready
by Al Lerner

© 2007 Al Lerner

All rights reserved.
No part of this book may be reproduced in any form or by any means, electronic, mechanical, digital, photocopying or recording, except for the inclusion in a review, without permission in writing from the the publisher.

www.Bearmanormedia.com
1-800-566-1251 (Order line only)

ISBN10: 1-59393-080-1
ISBN13: 978-1-59393-080-6

Printed in the United States

Book Design and Typesetting by Jill Ronsley, suneditwrite.com
Cover Design by Paula Tarver-Lecky & Jill Ronsley, Sun Editing & Book Design

Published in the USA by Bear Manor Media
PO Box 71426
Albany, GA 31708

Dedication

To my mother, Jennie, who introduced me to the piano.
To Ruth, who lived the life, and
To Jonne', who believed it was worth writing down

Contents

Acknowledgments	7
"Vamp 'Til Ready"	9
Prelude to a Life	11
Opening Chorus	19
Band on the Run	45
The Boys in the Band	47
Dick Haymes	49
The War Years	61
Glen Mccarthy	65
Hadacol Caravan	67
Howard Hughes	75
Frankie Laine	77
Buddy Rich	91
Al Martino	93
Rudy Vallee	95
George Gobel	99
Joan Crawford	107
Jimmy Doolittle	111
Marie "The Body" Mcdonald	115
Allan "Hello Mudda" Sherman	123
Shani Wallis & Richard Pryor	127

Tony Martin	129
Eddie Fisher	135
Australia Glenn Miller	139
Coda to a Full Life	141

Acknowledgments

Without a doubt this book could never have happened if not for the enduring belief in its value by my dear wife, Jonne'. Even though her professional life is busy and demanding, she always found the time to put all the stories I would tell her into writing. I appreciate the wisdom and intelligence she brings to everything she does. She is a tower of strength, and brings joy and love to my life every day. I also thank Ruth Prigozy, whose interest in my book brought it to completion. She was an endless source of encouragement and direction. Without her rallying for me, this book would not have been published. And finally a huge thanks to Ben Ohmart whose good humor and wisdom in the publishing of my book have fulfilled my wish to get these stories in print.

"Vamp 'Til Ready"

An expression that has been used since the beginning of old time vaudeville and burlesque. When the performer is announced, and the music starts to bring him on stage, if the applause still persisted by the time he/she reached center stage, the band or pianist played the two-bar phrase over and over again until the applause died down and the singer/performer started his/her act. This two-bar phrase is indicated on every musician's part as "VAMP 'TIL READY." It is still used today to prepare an act to start.

Prelude to a Life

It's funny how life is: you're born, you live, you die, and somewhere in between you do what you've got to do. I became a musician, probably because I have a good ear and perhaps a little talent but mostly because we needed to eat. I was born in 1919. My father had died in the flu epidemic of 1917-18, so I arrived in the world without a father. My mother remarried a man who was to become the only father I ever knew. Abe Lerner was a sheet metal worker and made a handsome living building stills for the gangsters and bootleggers in Cleveland. I never knew as a kid that my dad made stills for booze; I was told they were for making buttermilk so I couldn't inadvertently get my dad into trouble.

During Prohibition, Cleveland was a wide-open town, much like Chicago. Our shop had a long driveway, and from the back of the shop Dad would load the stills onto the gangsters' trucks, camouflaging them with burlap and crates, so it resembled a produce truck. As soon as the boss man would pay my dad, my father would surreptitiously stuff the money into the pockets of my pants and send me scurrying home. I would go flying down the street as fast as I could to my mother with seven or eight hundred dollars at a time. Dad knew no one would suspect a seven-year-old kid of taking money for illegal merchandise.

On several occasions when the trucks pulled out of our driveway and into the street, there was a barrage of gunfire from the Tommy guns of rival gangsters. In a matter of minutes the streets would be strewn with dead bodies, and sewers would literally run red with their blood. Then, as if choreographed, the cops would arrive, bang dents into the stills with their hammers for everyone to see, confiscate and impound the stills and pick up the bodies, in that order. It was all so crazy, like a Max Sennett comedy, only it wasn't funny. A few days later my parents and I would pay our respects to our former customers at various funeral parlors. The bodies were lying in coffins, the bullet holes in their faces stuffed with putty, and the coffins surrounded by floral tributes sent by their assassins. Calling these years the Roaring Twenties was quite an understatement!

About a week later my mother and Lt. Clemens from the "Roaring Third" precinct would do their little act. Clemens would saunter into our shop and casually tell my mom, "The stuff is in the yard." Mom would hand him some money, and Dad would pound the dents out of the stills and sell them again to the next gang. One day the Feds, posing as bootleggers new to the business, came into the shop and asked my Dad how to make mash, which is the basis for booze. Not suspecting a trap, he told them, and before he finished he was arrested, handcuffed, and taken down to the station house. I don't know what happened there, except that he paid a fine and was "out of business." From then on everything was downhill. Merchants Savings Bank collapsed and what few dollars we had in savings evaporated and we were flat broke.

My first foray into showbiz was when I was five years old. My best friend, Dave Ennis, and I stood on top of the tables in a swinging door saloon and sang, "All Alone by the Telephone." The patrons were kind enough to throw coins on the table. When I was six or seven, my mother bought a piano for my sister, Fay, but she had no interest in music whatsoever. This cleared the way for me to take piano lessons. I went to a convent next to St. Anne's Hospital, where I was born, to study with Sister Maria Concetta. As soon as I had to play with both hands, I quit. I thought it was just too hard.

My mother took me to see shows at the Palace, and one time, Bill Robinson was performing; I was hooked. Suddenly I wanted to be a hoofer, so I took tap dancing lessons from Roy Lewis, who taught many of the stars of the day. Pretty soon I was winning prizes and trophies at amateur night contests. I had dreams of tapping my way to stardom.

Jennie, my mother, always loved music and had a good ear. During the depths of the Depression, when we didn't know where our next

Vamp 'Til Ready

meal would come from, Mom always scraped up money for my lessons and my tap shoes. She never asked me to forgo a lesson or my practice to get a job and help out. She even saved a few pennies so we could stop and have a hot fudge sundae at Hoffman's Ice Cream Parlor. Those were special days and special times.

I've always suffered from shpilkas, which is Yiddish for "ants in your pants." I had then, as I do now, a great tendency to be restless. I like to be moving, doing, thinking, planning; I've never been content to just sit around. This trait did not necessarily serve me well during my school years. I was bored most of the time in classes, and never exhibited a bit of patience with kids who took longer to grasp the lessons. Instead of sitting quietly, I would clown around and act up, and eventually end up in the principal's office.

My older brother, Harold "Ace" Lerner, was a drummer. When I was thirteen, he gave me a set of drums and got me started on the basics. I took off from there. By the time I was fifteen I had my first paying job working with a trio in a local house of ill repute. I got the tidy sum of a $1.50 a night. What a thrill to take the money I had earned home to my mom, I was finally contributing something, and little did I know these were the humble beginnings of my career in music. I'll never forget the night the saxophone player's father came in the front door, his mouth fell open, his face turned scarlet, but it was too late to turn and run, one of life's embarrassing moment for everyone concerned. To make matters worse, his father tried to stammer his way out of the predicament by saying that he had an appointment but went to the wrong address.

One freezing night in Cleveland, it dawned on me that the piano player only had to put on his coat and gloves and then split. I had drums to pack up and lug home on the trolley. I knew then it was time to go back to the piano. I began my piano studies in earnest with my cousin and soon after was playing joints in Cleveland. My first job was at Shadowland, where the entertainment consisted of waitresses who doubled as strippers and my trio: piano, sax and drums. Our hours were nine to two-thirty in the morning and we played for a princely sum of fifteen bucks a week. I learned to play jazz by listening to Earl Hines records. I also learned that if I turned off the motor of my Model

Al Lerner

A Ford and coasted down Carnegie Avenue, I could get to work and back on ten cents worth of gas.

One night after work, a local bass player asked me to go with him after work to a little joint on Cedar Avenue, the Harlem of Cleveland. Val's in the Alley was like no other ginmill with music I had ever been in. There was a single light bulb dangling from a pipe that barely illuminated the door. Customers walked up a little stoop and into the darkest and smokiest joint in Cleveland. Sitting over in the corner was an old, and I do mean old, beat up upright piano, with nobody playing it. There were only a few people sitting around at that hour of the morning, so my so-called friend said, "Al, why don't you go over and play a couple of tunes?" Cocky kid that I was, I said to myself, "why not?" and strode over to the piano, sat down and with all the sophistication of a seventeen-year-old, played "Rosetta" in my best Earl Hines imitation. I followed with a couple of other tunes, then feeling pretty smug, with a smirk on my face, I returned to the table to finish my beer. I even had the gall to look around the room to see if anyone had heard me, as only the young and uninitiated are brazen enough to do. It was then that I noticed a hulk of a man standing by the small, homemade, makeshift bar, looking up at the ceiling and drinking beer. Quietly and deliberately, he walked over to the piano, set down his beer and struck a chord. That's all I had to hear to know I was dead. That chord was like nothing I had ever heard before; it made the hair stand up on the back of my neck. Then he played "Tea for Two" like I had never heard it played it before.

Humiliated, I ran out of the club and down the alley crying like a baby. Red, the bass player, ran after me and apologized for setting me up, and asked me to come back into the club, because the piano man who had just blown me away wanted to meet me. Mustering up every bit of courage I could, I returned to meet Art Tatum.

"Kid, I like your style," he said. "Come here as often as you can and sit in." My heart leaped into my mouth, and I struggled to whisper thanks. This was to become the beginning of a great friendship that lasted the rest of his life. If Art and I were in the same town at the same time, I moved heaven and earth to see him. Pianistically, he was God. The last time I saw Art was at the Swing Club in Hollywood. Frankie

Laine, his wife Nan, Ruth, my late wife, and I went there to celebrate our wedding anniversaries, which fell on the same day. Art told his two side men to take five, and played alone for us the rest of the night. Anyone who's heard Art recognized it as a rare privilege and a feast for the ears and soul. Little did I know that this would be one of the last times I would see him. He died shortly after the age of fifty-six, but left a big hole in my heart and an even bigger musical legacy.

Art Tatum was truly a musical jazz genius. He was without peer. What made his jazz so outstanding probably was due to the fact that he studied classical piano for thirteen years. Every pianist in the field of modern piano artistry can thank Art Tatum for evoking creativity in every one of us. We only wish we could play half as good as he did. To this day, no pianist has approached what Art could create in the moment. When I sit down and play, sometimes I come up with something new and fresh off the top of my head, and I wonder if Art would let out a "yeah." Sadly, my friend, my inspiration, my mentor died of kidney failure. I could not cry, it hurt so bad.

By the time I was seventeen years old, I was working in joints around Cleveland for fifteen bucks a week. That was a lot of money in 1937. I was gaining some notoriety as a local jazz musician, earning the respect of my peers. During a visit with relatives in Detroit, I heard a band out of Texas led by Ben Young. Gordon "Tex" Beneke, Claude Lakey, and Dalton Rosatti were members of the band, and we struck up a friendship. A few weeks later, when they were playing in Cleveland, they stopped by Shadowland to see me. Claude and Dalton were on their way to New York to join the newly organized Harry James Band. About a year later, the James Band came to The Trianon Ballroom in Cleveland with a new singer by the name of Frank Sinatra. Wow, was he something! He was fresh and exciting and brought a whole new approach to singing with a band. The next time I saw the James Band was when they came to town to play for prom night at the Cleveland Hotel. The boy singer was Dick Haymes, who had replaced Sinatra. My old friend Claude Lakey invited me to come and hear the band and their new singer. Claude asked Harry if I could sit in because he wanted Harry to hear me play. I played a set with the band as soon as I finished, Harry asked me if I would like to join the band. I could hardly

Al Lerner

control myself, I was so excited, but I managed to blurt out "When?" "Tonight," said Harry. I immediately backed off, because I didn't want to leave my girl. So I told Harry I couldn't join him at that time.

Harry and the boys

Shortly after Harry James left town, I was offered an engagement in Florida with a fine singer named Kirk Wood, who sang with many bands of the forties, Alvino Ray, Little Jack Little and more. Kirk and I took off with a boyhood friend, Irv Metzenbaum, brother of Howard, who would go on to become one of the most powerful senators in Washington, and my good buddy, Vic Corpora, in Irv's 1938 Pontiac. Vic was a wonderful drummer and lyricist that wrote the lyrics to my music, "So Until I See You," which was chosen by Jack Paar to be the closing theme for his *Tonight Show*.

On the way down, we stopped in St. Augustine, Florida so I could visit Ponce DeLeon's fountain of youth and purchase a bottle of water for my girlfriend, Ruth, who was all of seventeen years old and hardly in need of a youth elixir.

Then on to Miami. When we arrived in there we had to find a place to stay. We started looking around Miami Beach, but quickly found out we couldn't afford to stay there. So we began to look around Miami for a rooming house, and found one we could afford. The $2.50 rate for two in a room was well within our means. Planted firmly on the front lawn was a sign that proclaimed for everyone to see "No Dogs or Jews"! We had so little money that I had to overlook the bigotry. We rented the room. I wonder if they ever knew a Jew slept in their precious bed. We found a place to eat a seven-course meal for thirty-five cents. We had it made, or at least we thought so. We reported for work only to find out that the job had fallen through. So we decided to go to Havana. Why? Because we'd never been there. Kirk found work singing in a local club and decided stay behind. The trip to Havana on the good ship The Cuba was a nightmare. The ship tossed and turned in the rough seas all night long, and we spent the time heaving over the railing, wishing we were dead. The next morning twelve of the two-hundred passengers showed up in the dining room, but only four ate breakfast. How did I know this? I was one of the four who, along with Irv, ate that morning.

We landed in Havana and set ourselves up in a cheap hotel. We had no money for booze and food, so we visited the local rum distilleries, tossing down the free samples offered to tourists in the hopes that they would purchase the rum and take it back to the States in their luggage. We heard about a famous bar in Havana called Sloppy Joes. It was crummy looking, dank and dreary and filled with tourists, who like us, wondered why they had gone out of their way to visit it. Soon our Cuban holiday was over and we headed back to Miami on *The Cuba*, this time with the contents of our stomachs intact.

Landing in Miami, I called my mother, who told me there had been several calls from someone named Jimmy Harry. "Do you mean Harry James?" I asked, and she said "Yes, that's it." My heart leaped. It was pretty exciting to think someone as famous has Harry James wanted to talk to me. Jumping in the Pontiac, we drove straight home, stopping only for gas. Food was out of the question; we were too broke to eat.

I was in love with Ruth, the recipient of the fountain of youth water, and I wanted to see how she felt about me before I made a decision about going to New York to join the James Band. So in a friend's borrowed car, I took Ruth for a drive and summoning up all my courage, I said, "Ruth, what's the score?" Not knowing what I was trying to ask her, she said, "I know the Indians played today, but I don't know the score." I clarified my position, and she said, "I don't think so." I now knew where I stood and decided right then and there to call Harry and join the band, and in fact I did just that. I left the next day for New York and the beginning of my lifelong career in music.

Louise Tobin

Opening Chorus

Harry booked a room for me at the Forrest Hotel on Forty-ninth Street. Lots of guys from the bands lived there who were working around Mid-Manhattan. I was pretty much a greenhorn from Cleveland, so it was comforting for me to be around my peers, many of whom I only knew by reputation. They became my extended family, and some of those friendships have endured throughout my life.

The Harry James Band was working at The Chatterbox in Plainfield, New Jersey, a typical roadside joint, run by hoods and frequented by more of the same and their molls. The first night Harry himself drove me out to the club in his car. I thought it was pretty terrific that Harry James was driving me, Al Lerner, to my first date with the band. When we arrived at the club, I was surprised and bewildered to find the piano player I was supposed to be replacing was on the bandstand at the piano. There was Jumbo Jack Gardner, all 450 pounds of him sitting on stage ready to play the first set. Harry said, "You'll play the second set." This was a very curious situation and I couldn't figure what was going on.

Naively, I asked Jack, "When are you leaving the band?"

"I have no plans to leave the band," he said.

Now I was really confused, what the hell was going on? Not one to second guess, I went to Harry during the intermission, and asked him what he had in mind for me.

"I'm going to have two pianos in the band."

Strange, I thought, and I wasn't too sure I believed a word he had just said. There had never been a swing band with two pianos; I knew that just wouldn't work. But here I was in New York, this was my first big break, and who was I to argue with the leader. Harry said he wanted to break me in with the band and he gave Jack the rest of the engagement off.

The Chatterbox was one of those colorful dives that Damon Runyon wrote so eloquently about. The "patrons" of the club were pretty rough characters. While we played in the front, the real action was taking place in the "back room." Thick with smoke doesn't begin to describe what it was like in there. The room was filled with gamblers, smoking everything that could be lit up and inhaled. We used to go upstairs to the lounge between sets and play cards.

One night, Jack Palmer, one of the trumpet players, lagged behind to clean up the table, and was late getting back, and Harry started the set without him. Harry was never known as a smooth talker or even a nice guy by those who knew him. Angrily, Harry chewed out Jack in front of everyone, band and customers alike. Jack attempted to explain, but Harry wouldn't let up.

Jack, setting his horn in his lap, stared Harry right in the eye and said, "Why don't you stick your sarcastic tongue up your ass."

Harry snapped back at Jack and told him he wanted to see him after the set.

Jack, who was not one to be intimidated by anyone, least of all Harry James, shot back with, "I'll see you in the parking lot." Jack wasn't the type of guy you wanted to meet in a parking lot, and Harry was no exception.

Harry quickly took stock of the situation, and said, "Let's have a drink after the set."

Jack said, "Get lost," finished the set and gave his notice that night.

Harry had a way with the guys; this is just one example of how he alienated nearly everyone around him.

Vamp 'Til Ready

Playing the Paramount in 1940

An engagement at the Paramount Theater in New York followed, featuring Bea Wain, whose recording "My Reverie" with Larry Clinton was a hit of the day. Here we were, still with two pianos, and I'm still trying to figure out what Harry is up to. Each day that passed I became more uneasy with the situation as Jack and I were becoming pretty good friends. Jack was a real likeable guy, and was as confused over this as I was; we discussed our dilemma at great length. Jack was becoming more depressed every day, and growing increasingly uncomfortable, began drinking more than usual. At The Chatterbox, Jack and I shared one piano, alternating sets. At the Paramount, Harry had two pianos set at opposite ends of the stage. The night we opened, Harry gave Jack all the music for the show. The opener for the show was an arpeggio to bring on Bea Wain singing "My Reverie." Harry gave Jack the cue to start the arpeggio, and nothing happened. Dead silence! He looked over to the piano where Jack was seated to find that Jack was slumped over the keyboard out cold. I quickly picked up that there was a problem and gave the arpeggio, my heart in the mouth, not really knowing for sure if I should go ahead without Harry's cue. Immediately, the music was picked up off Jack's piano and passed through the band to me and I played the rest of the show. We ended the show with "Chiribiribin," Harry's theme song. I breathed a sigh of relief, followed by utter despair and frustration over what had just happened and the uncertainty of it all. The stage slowly sank to the basement and my spirits sank with it. Jack had remained lifeless, slumped over the keyboard, dead drunk, during the entire show.

Jack weighed 450 pounds. We now had to figure out how we were going to get him out of the pit. The orchestra pit of the Paramount also had a riser with a huge Wurlitzer Organ on it.

The job was to carry a 450-pound man past the organ and through a small narrow door, just big enough for one man to exit at a time. Several of the biggest and most able-bodied guys picked Jumbo Jack up and carrying him safari style, and wedged him through the passageway sideways, and took him upstairs to the band room on the backstage elevator. In a couple of days Jack was gone, no goodbyes, no explanations, nothing, he was just gone. We never heard another word, but I guess Harry, in his inimitable way, had fired Jack, or at the very least made his life so miserable that he had to leave the band.

Jack's departure meant that I was now the pianist with the Harry James Band. My big break! Ha! I had a pretty good idea of what kind of guy Harry James was, and now I had to figure out how to please him musically and maintain my anonymity.

I had left my girlfriend Ruth in Cleveland; thankfully she had a change of heart and came to New York with my mother to patch things up, so we decided it was time to get married. We planned our wedding for a weekend I knew I had off. I flew home on Friday night, and was married on Sunday and my bride and I hopped a plane to New York that night. I had to be in New York to open the next night at the Lincoln Hotel. I was more than anxious to get home to my bride, so after we completed our opening that Monday night, I hurriedly packed up my music and started to dash off the bandstand. Harry stopped me and said, "There's a rehearsal tonight." I stopped dead in my tracks, and with a heavy heart, turned to walk back to the piano. Everyone knew about the rehearsal but me, as I had been out of town getting married over the weekend.

We set up to start, and Harry called out a few numbers and stood there silently. Slyly, he turned and said, "Okay, Al, go home, just kidding." I flew off the stage and down the street to my hotel to begin my life with Ruth.

We finished the two-week engagement and out next stop was at the Hippodrome in Baltimore. There was a young unknown singer who joined us there. Little did we know that she would go to become the highest paid and most popular singers in the era of the big movie musicals. Her name was Betty Hutton. The boy singer with Harry was Dick Haymes. I was settling in the band, and Dick and I were becoming good friends. We roomed together; single rooms were more that a musician's pay would cover. Dick was getting forty-five dollars a week and I was getting seventy-five a week at that time. Before going to bed, I would dump my money out of my pocket and put it on the night stand between the two beds. In the morning, Dick would always call up for room service and when the food arrived, he signed for his meal and tipped the porter from my stash on the night stand. A portent of things to come! At the end of every week, Dick never had enough and sometimes no money to cover his bill, and Harry would bail him out. I didn't know that this was Dick's m.o. and he would do this the rest of his life. I also didn't know then that our lives would become intertwined for many more years.

Next up, Flushing Meadows — The World's Fair. We were the featured band at Mike Todd's "Dancing Campus," an outdoor dance floor. We alternated with the Les Brown Band, Bob Chester and Mike Riley. Mike Riley was famous for writing the hit song "The Music Goes Round and Round," a smash for that era, staying on the Hit Parade for many weeks. We were in good company. Dinah Shore used to come by to hear Dick. Dick was the best singer of that time. Even though that is my personal opinion, most of the vocal artists of that period shared my view.

Al Lerner

We lived in Manhattan at the Forrest Hotel, and took the "A" train out to the Meadows. Yes, that's the very same train immortalized by Duke Ellington. Our engagement lasted a month. One weekend Harry got the bright idea of having a Judy Garland sound-alike contest. He chose the hottest two days of the summer of 1940. I accompanied about 120 would-be singers over those two days, sitting under a blazing sun from noon to sundown, wearing a suit and a tie. I was burned to a crisp, blistered and raw with heat rash. Most of the renditions that day by amateurs were pretty horrible. I still get prickly heat whenever I hear "Babes in Arms" or "Over the Rainbow."

Me in 1940

We left for Detroit after we closed at the Fair to play at Eastwood Gardens, an amusement park that featured the big swing bands of that time. Bob Crosby, Woody Herman, Les Brown, Benny Goodman, Artie Shaw and many more all came there. Now I had only been with the band for six months, and most of the guys were from Texas. I felt a little like an outsider, no drawl, certainly not a redneck, and no inside track with Harry, who was also a Texan. I didn't even know where the Alamo was.

The guitar player, Red Kent, was one of Harry's buddies from Texas. He rubbed me the wrong way from the moment I joined the band. It was mutual, we couldn't stand each other. Every time I had a solo, he would put his guitar down, cross his arms over his chest and stare straight ahead, as if I or my music didn't exist. As soon as I realized what was happening, I followed him into the band room after we finished the set.

Walking up to him, I asked, "Why don't you play during my solo?"

He shot back, "I don't understand those chords you play."

"What do you mean, don't you have an ear, or can't you hear?" I snarled. I continued on with, "Oh, I guess it's pretty hard to duplicate what I'm playing on a four-string guitar. Oh, I see you have a six-string guitar."

The entire scene had just been witnessed by the entire band, including Harry. The silence was deafening. I turned around and stomped out of the band room. I called home to Cleveland that night and told the family my career in music was probably over and I most likely would be home in two or three weeks.

We went on to Boston and a run at the Brunswick Hotel the next day, no one mentioning the "incident." We were staying at the Touraine Hotel, which was famous for being the favorite haunt of the great names in the theatre. The Barrymores were among its most notable guests, along with Lunt & Fontanne, and Katharine Cornell. We did a "remote" broadcast every night during our show at the Roof Garden of the Brunswick. The day before we opened, Harry called a rehearsal and balance check for the radio station. When we finished, Harry started out of the room, then stopped, made a quarter turn, and with all the warmth of an iceberg, announced, "I want everyone to have brown shoes for tomorrow's opening. Oh, and by the way, some of you will find notices in your box tomorrow morning." We all sat there stunned, no one moved or uttered word; it was one of life's dreadful moments. Then silently, everyone filed from the band room, eyes cast down and filled with trepidation.

I knew for sure I would be going. After all, I wasn't from Texas, one of the good ol' boys; I was just the new kid on the stand, and a pretty assertive one at that. I didn't take any lip, period, I didn't care who you were, and I had just confronted Harry's friend from Texas on the bandstand in front of everyone, and that included Harry himself. I was a goner. Once we caught our breath and found our voices, Vido Musso, a well-known and popular tenor sax man, Mickey Scrima, drummer, and Dick Haymes and I decided to go to Scolly Square to a cheap movie. Later we sat down to talk about our fate. Like me, they thought they would be on the noon train. Dick owned Harry money. Vido was having a hard time in the sax section, and Mickey was constantly getting the "ray" from Harry. We all came to the same conclusion; we had no immediate prospects of another job, we had to sweat it out.

The day wasn't a total loss. On the way back to the hotel, I ran into my good friend, Red Norvo, the great vibraharpist. It was his birthday, so he asked me to come back to his room for drink before I turned in. "What the hell," I thought. "I might as well enjoy my last night with the James Band with a drink and a friend." As we passed the front desk, the clerk called Red over to give him a package from Mildred Bailey, who was Red's wife. Mildred was one of the great blues singers of thirties and forties. The birthday "present" was a new suit. I put the word present in quotes, because Red's gift was sent C.O.D. I still laugh out loud as Red and I did that evening when I think of his birthday suit.

Dick and I roomed together at the Touraine on this tour, and silently we fell into our beds, neither one of us mentioning the "incident." The next morning Dick came over to my bed and tapped me on the shoulder and with all the nonchalance he could muster, said, "Shall I see if we got any mail?" With a well-rehearsed air of casual indifference, Dick called down to the desk, and asked, "Is there anything in our mailbox?" After what seemed like an eternity, Dick looked at me in amazement and said, "There's nothing in the box!" I looked back, stunned, sighed in relief, and rolled over and went back to sleep.

Later that morning, we remembered Harry's edict about the brown shoes, and ran out of the hotel to find the cheapest pair of brown shoes in Boston. We paid three bucks for a pair of Thom McCann brown brogans, and went to work. As we sat on the bandstand that night, trying to play our sets, an uneasy air of expectation hung over the band. No one was asking anyone if they had gotten their notice. The roaring silence was finally broken by Red Kent, who just couldn't stand it any longer. Turning to me and dripping with sarcasm, he said, "Well, did you get anything in your box today?" Sheepishly, I said "no." I was floored when he said, "Well, I did." As it turned out Mr. Nice Guy, Harry James had fired most of his buddies from Texas. There was no accounting for Harry's actions.

Before we left this engagement, a whole new group of men had come into replace Dave Mathews, Truett Jones, and Red Kent. They were Hoyt Bohannon, Bennie Heller, and Johnny Mezey. These men were among my dearest friends. Johnny, Bennie and Hoyt were probably the finest musicians I have ever had the privilege to work with. Hoyt's mastery of the trombone was legendary and earned the respect of everyone in the business. Johnny Mezey played tenor sax with Red Norvo's Band and also with Raymond Scott. He was, in my estimation, one of the most talented and innovative musicians I have ever known. He played softly and masterfully, and when he played you listened. His talents were not limited to music. In between shows he would go back to his hotel room and paint beautiful watercolor pictures. Poor Johnny died when he was only forty-eight from a bad case of the flu which turned into pneumonia. I still miss him.

Bennie Heller came to us from the Benny Goodman Band. He had just won the *Downbeat* poll. *Downbeat* was a monthly magazine that listed the whereabouts of every band, who was in and who was out. Annually they conducted a poll among their readers asking them to name their favorite artists. Winning was indeed an honor, and Bennie was so honored. He played the guitar and was truly a gifted musician. My great and good friend Bennie died in 1982 and, like Johnny, I miss him.

Hoyt was one of those special guys. He was quiet and unassuming and an absolute genius. The sound that he could coax out of his trombone could melt your heart and make you want to stand up and cheer at the same time. Hoyt would go into a job and just sit down in the section, never taking the first chair. The first chair in a section is reserved for the "stars" or the lead player. Once, Hoyt was sent to Warner Bros. to play for Max Steiner, a wonderful composer and famous conductor in movies. Hoyt went into the studio, quietly sat down, and waited. Max had written a piece that had a rather difficult part for trombone. The lead trombone man got up and tried the part, couldn't play it, the second chair tried and failed, then the third. Finally, Max turned to Hoyt and said, "Would you like to try?" Hoyt nodded, stood up, and on the first attempt, without ever having seen the part before, played it flawlessly. From that day on Max Steiner never recorded without Hoyt. My great and good friend died years ago and in tribute, trombone players meet at his house once a week in his studio to practice and play. Most will remember Harry's recording of "Sleepy Lagoon," and Hoyt's beautiful trombone solo.

Now it was time to move onto Chicago for an engagement at the Panther Room in the Hotel Sherman. The day of our opening, I showed up at a rehearsal in a yellow sport shirt. As soon as I reached the bandstand Harry's eyes flew open and he said, "What are you wearing?" Before I could reply I was jumped by three guys in the band, wrestled to the ground and my shirt was literally ripped off my back, and torn into a mass of shreds. No one had told me that we were never to wear yellow around Harry. He had a superstition about the color yellow. I don't know why to this day, but, as far as Harry was concerned, it was taboo.

Edith Harper was the singer on the bill along with Dick. Dick took her out and two weeks later she was the first in a series of Mrs. Dick Haymeses. During our run at the Panther Room, Victor Mature came in one night with Betty Gable, a stunning blonde, with beautiful legs and a gorgeous figure, and sat at a table very close to the band. They were on a promotional tour for the movie *One Million B.C.* Harry was invited to the table to meet Vic and was introduced to Betty. Harry was a pretty tough guy to read, he didn't give himself away, but that night there wasn't doubt among any of us in the band that Harry had flipped. He was married at the time to Louise Tobin, a singer who had been with Benny Goodman. Louise was pretty damn gorgeous too, and she and Harry had two sons together. Harry and Betty's paths didn't cross again until one night about two years later. This time Harry didn't waste a moment and Betty Gable became Mrs. Harry James shortly after Louise and Harry's divorce became final. Louise subsequently married

Vamp 'Til Ready

a friend of mine, "Peanuts Hucko," one of the premier clarinetists, and had a long and happy marriage with him.

The two weeks at the Panther Room were uneventful, even though Dick married Edith and Harry met Betty. We were all looking forward to our next date at the Paramount Theater in New York. Co-starring with the James Band were Peter Lind Hayes, Mary Healy, and Frank Parker. Rehearsals were set for seven every morning in the rehearsal hall of the Paramount. As soon as we finished, we'd all go back to the hotel, jump back in bed, and forget what we had just rehearsed, trusting that Harry would save us during the performance. Harry had the uncanny ability to remember every cue, tempo and entrance. The morning of our opening, we rehearsed as was our custom, and immediately went back to bed. The first show was at eleven that morning. I was rooming with "Bones" Bohannan at the time, and we were both sound asleep at the Piccadilly Hotel. The Pick, as we called it, was located right across the alley from the Paramount, in fact the front entrance of the hotel opened onto Shubert's Alley. I was rudely awakened by the shrill ringing of the bedside phone. Our band boy, Al Monte, was frantically screaming at me over the wire, "You're on in four minutes!" I lunged from my bed, shoving my feet into my shoes, while grabbing and snatching for pieces of my uniform. I yanked my pants on, and as I bolted toward the door. Snatching my jacket from the chair, I shook Hoyt and yelled in his ear, "We're on in four minutes. I'm going and goodbye." As I fled from the room, I saw Hoyt turn over and go back to sleep, nothing I had said registered. As I ran through the alley trying to pull myself together, I realized that I wasn't wearing socks, and I didn't have my shirt or tie. But the show must go on, so I just kept running toward the theater. I ran into the backstage area and over to the elevator, which took the band up on the hydraulic stage. I got there as the stage was beginning its ascent to the proscenium level. I leapt up, grabbed the leg of the piano, pulling myself with all my might onto the stage. I crawled onto the piano bench and sat down just as Harry gave the downbeat. This wouldn't have been so bad if the first number hadn't been a big piano solo, but as luck would have it, the spotlight was on me. What a pathetic sight. There I was shirtless, sock-less, unshaven, hair uncombed, my hairy chest exposed, playing

"Flash." Apropos of the moment! Harry turned and cast his eyes of Texas upon me, and nearly flipped. Harry, cool as ever, never skipped a beat, as if nothing out of the ordinary had taken place. Right in the middle of our show I heard a commotion at the back of the stage. Hoyt had finally showed up! The stagehands had put up a ladder so Hoyt could climb onto the stage and join the trombone section. Hoyt was one of the most relaxed guys I have ever known. Nothing ever seemed to bother him. He had one speed, his. He could tune out the world. As was his trademark, Hoyt joined the band as if nothing unusual had just happened. His big solo number in "Sleepy Lagoon" was next. All horn players have to warm up before they play and Hoyt was no exception. Needless to say, he had not warmed up. As soon as he settled into the section, the spotlight fell on him; Hoyt casually stood up, lifted his trombone to his lips and blew. Silence! Absolutely nothing came out of his horn that morning that even remotely resembled music, just the sound of a thin stream of air in a hollow tube. The band fell apart and one by one began laughing. Even the audience joined in that day. Hoyt, however, took it all in stride, the band played on, because, after all, the show must go on.

On our next date at the Paramount, Ray Bolger was billed as the feature act with the band. The morning of our first rehearsal with Ray, I started to mimic Ray. I had once harbored the hope of being a hoofer; at the age of five I gave up the piano to take tap dancing lessons. This cracked Ray up, and he thought it would be a great idea to have a challenge dance in the show. A challenge dance is when the star does a step or two and the other performer does the same steps and adds another one or tops the star and so on. Even though I said no, that I was just kidding around, Ray persisted and it went into the show. Ray would come out onto the stage, start dancing and from the piano I would make a gesture that would convey to the audience that I was putting him down. Ray would come over to the piano and pull me off the bench and dare me to do the same steps. It became a real hit with the audience, and we were doing it at all five shows during the week and seven shows on weekends. My ankles swelled, my feet were so sore I had to soak them every night just to keep going. I made a wise decision after that engagement, stick to the piano.

Ray Bolger and me dancing on stage
at the Paramount Theatre in New York, 1941

During this run, one Sunday afternoon, the management came on stage to announce that President Roosevelt would be speaking to us over the P.A. system. A hush fell over the theater as the President told us the Japanese had just attacked Pearl Harbor. At the conclusion of his speech, everyone sat completely motionless, when Ray Bolger ran over to the mike, and said, "If there are any Japs out there, come up on stage and I'll punch you in the nose." After a moment of stunned silence, the band softly began to play, and we went on with the show.

During the Paramount engagement, Ray and I became pretty good friends. Upon closing, I went to Ray's dressing room to tell him how much fun it was to dance and joke with him in our little act. He gave me a photo of himself, on which he wrote, "Thanks for helping me with my act."

Our paths didn't cross again for twenty-five years. One day in Sherman Oaks, I received a call from a young man, who asked if he could interview me. He was writing a piece for a magazine about Dick Haymes. He was most interested in my long relationship with Dick; thirteen years is a long time in show business.

The journalist asked me to meet him at the Tail O' Cock restaurant, in the bar. He also asked me to bring some photos, and I obliged. While sitting at the bar talking, he turned away and said, "Oh, look, there's Ray Bolger at that table." I turned to see Ray sitting with a small group of people, having a late lunch. I stared for a moment and then impulsively decided to walk over and speak to Ray. I excused myself from the young reporter, walked over and stood in front of the table.

The conversation stopped and Ray, not immediately recognizing me, asked politely, "What can we do for you?"

I looked straight at Ray and said, "I don't know if you remember, but I was the pianist with the Harry James Band that danced with you."

As soon as the words were out of my mouth, Ray sprang to his feet and hugged me, and said, "I sure do. Where have you been? What are you doing now?" – All in one breath.

He turned to his lunch companions and said to them, "Excuse me; I want to talk to Al."

He joined me at the bar, and I made another date with the reporter to finish the Haymes story. Ray and I began reminiscing and had more than a few laughs. After a couple of drinks, we jumped off the barstools and began to dance. The patrons of the restaurant went nuts; soon there was a crowd around us, laughing and clapping. The only thing missing were the dimes I used to get when I danced and sang as a kid during Prohibition at the local bar in Cleveland. Every time I hear "Over the Rainbow," I think of my old pal, The Scarecrow. He was a very special fellow. It was a day that shall live in my memory.

I have portrayed Harry as an uncaring, rather nasty fellow, because that pretty much says how I felt about him. But I cannot deny that he was a musical genius. He was uncanny. Without any warm-up, he could put his trumpet to his lips and blow you right out of your chair. His memory was perfect, he only had to hear an arrangement once, and he could retain it forever. The same with a printed score, he could glance at his part, and play it perfectly. That's some kind of ability.

Even though we were one of the most popular bands of the day, and working constantly, there was never enough money to cover everything. We leased a bus from Greyhound to take us on our tours, forty and fifty one-night stands. We had one special driver, Lenny, who we considered part of the band; we never thought of him as an employee of the bus company. Often, Harry couldn't pay for the bus,

Al Lerner

so when he would get behind, Greyhound would alert the police to detain us from leaving town until they got paid. Lenny didn't care one way or the other, and he had more fun with a crazy bunch of musicians than he did with most fares, so he would wait for us in an alley near the theater, and the band would quietly sneak out a door that didn't have police standing by and go to the bus. As soon as everyone was on and the instruments stowed, Lenny would pull out, taking every back alley and dirt road he knew to get us out of town. He never even turned on the headlights. So lest one gets the idea that being in the band was all fun and glamour, I am here to say that it had its dark moments as well as spectacular highs.

Harry was an avid baseball fan and loved to play the game. One of the prerequisites to joining his band was that you damn well better be able to play baseball as well as you played your instrument. Harry was such a "nut" about baseball that often while driving down the highway to our next engagement, Harry would tell Lenny to pull over, and we'd all have to get out of the bus and play baseball by the side of the highway. During one of our engagements at the Lincoln Hotel in New York, Tommy Dorsey's band was at the Astor Roof. The rivalry between the two bands wasn't limited to music; there was an ongoing contest on the baseball diamond as well. We used to meet in Central Park to play, and on several occasions went to Tommy's estate in Bernardsville, New Jersey. Tommy lived in a beautiful mansion with lush gardens, a tennis court, swimming pool, and lawns big enough for a baseball field. Tommy's team had Frank Sinatra, Buddy Rich, Bunny Berigan, the Pied Pipers, and Ziggy Elman, to name a few. Bunny was the home plate umpire. He would stand behind the batters with his chest protector, glove, and a pocketful of Dixie cups in his back pocket. In another pocket was a bottle of gin, and between every pitch, Bunny would toss down a cup of gin. By the third inning he couldn't even see the batter in front of him, let alone the ball. It made for some very interesting calls. These outings were a gas for a lot of the guys who, like me, grew up struggling through the Depression, to be on an estate like this. Tommy was a great host and treated us to a great day of fun, food, booze, and we always had a great game of baseball. These were wonderful times.

Our band had about eighteen guys, all of whom were expected to play baseball as well as their axe. We would often play games in Central Park, choosing up sides from among ourselves.

I was a pretty good southpaw pitcher, so I pitched. Harry was not only the leader of the band, but also he assumed the same role on the baseball diamond. We could always count on Harry to hit the ball when we were in the clutch. Harry's team and my team were playing a close ball game that day, and we were all tied-up in the eight inning. I was on the mound, I pitched a low insider, and Harry hit a grounder right back to me. I scooped the ball off the ground, and hurled it to first base and he slid in. It was close, but he was out. Harry had other ideas. Ignoring the call, Harry got up, brushed himself off and stood on the bag.

I looked over from the mound in amazement, and said, "Harry, you're out, what are doing there? Get off the base."

He shot back with, "I'm safe."

I said, "You're out."

With that, Harry turned to the first baseman, Al Friede, our Cello player, and with eyes of steel said to him, "Al, am I out?"

Al meekly stuttered back, "I think you're safe."

I threw down my glove, and said, "Well, you're the leader on the ball field too." I walked off the field and never played baseball with Harry again. It's a good thing he liked the way I played piano, as that was grounds for dismissal. Harry was one tough act.

Glenn Miller enlisted in the Army, leaving an opening on the *Chesterfield Hour*, a radio show that aired on Tuesday, Wednesday and Thursday of every week. The James Band was chosen to replace the Miller Band because we had just been named number one band in the land. This meant an increase in our salaries. My new wife and I had been housing and feeding two out of work friends from Cleveland in a one bedroom apartment on seventy-five bucks a week. No mean feat. I would now be making three hundred dollars a week. This was a small fortune to a couple of kids from Ohio. We were so used to scrimping and making do, nothing really changed except that I could send more money home to my mother, and Ruth could afford to buy some new clothes.

Al Lerner

With Harry and the band, May 9, 1943

The Chesterfield Show was our springboard into films. We were called to do a movie at Universal titled *Private Buckaroo*; it was so bad that the guys renamed it "Private Stinkeroo"! I saw it not too long ago on TV, it was pretty horrible. Harry had us go to the coast by train, because he refused to fly. We'd leave on Friday, get to Los Angeles on Monday morning and go straight to the set. After shooting our scenes all day, we'd go right from the studio to the *Chesterfield Show,* which had moved to Hollywood, do the fifteen-minute show, with a repeat. In those days there was no tape, we had to do them live twice a day, one for the West Coast and one for the East Coast. We finished up about seven-thirty, and went straight to the Palladium and played until one o'clock in the morning. And the kids today think they have it tough. We were making lots of money, but who cared; nobody had time to spend any of it.

We were the hot band during that time and left L.A. after we finished *Private Buckaroo* for an engagement at the Astor Roof in New

Vamp 'Til Ready

York. We had a few hits at the time, "You Made Me Love You," "Sleepy Lagoon," "I Don't Want to Walk Without You," featuring Helen Forrest as vocalist. Harry and I wrote an instrumental called "Music Makers." Even though I got along with Harry, it does not negate my opinion of him, he could be a real louse. He took over the piece, as was his style, never gave me, or anyone else with whom he collaborated, credit when he published the tune. To make matters worse, it was one of the biggest instrumental records of that time. Harry had a proclivity for castigating and/or firing one of the guys in front of the whole band. This did not endear him to anyone, least of all my good friend Claude Lakey, a great all-around musician. Claude could play in practically every section of the band, trumpet, sax, lead alto, and tenor. One afternoon we were sitting around jamming, waiting for Harry to arrive and start the rehearsal. Lakey was standing up playing his alto as Harry strode in the room and said to him, "Okay, stupid, sit down." A hush fell over the bandstand, and we knew instantly that Harry was in one of his "moods." Lakey was a gentle giant of a fellow from Texas. Without a word, he sat down and we started to rehearse the program. After about an hour, Harry called a break and went into his dressing room just off the stage. Lakey and I walked off the stage together toward Harry's dressing room. Lakey stopped at Harry dressing room and, poking his head around the door, asked Harry is he could see him a moment. Without skipping a beat, Harry said, "Sure, Lakey, come on in"; it was pretty obvious that Harry had forgotten his remarks to Claude earlier.

I outside the door, and as I waited for Claude, I heard him say, "Harry, do you remember saying, 'Okay, sit down, stupid' to me?'" Harry was at a loss for words, he had no explanation. Lakey shot back with, "Harry, don't ever say that to me again, 'cause I'll break your fucking back," and turned and walked out.

With Harry James and Nancy Walker in the early 1940s

One afternoon during rehearsal Harry stopped the band about eight bars into the number, looked directly at Mickey Scrima, our drummer, and said, "You play louder than Buddy Rich and Gene Krupa together." I got that sinking feeling that this was going to be curtains for good buddy Mickey. Harry beat off the number again, and this time four bars into the tune, Harry stopped, looked at Mickey, and said, "Just pack up your drums and get the hell out of here." When Mickey said, "What about the show?," Harry, in his most vitriolic manner, said, "I don't care if we do the show without drums." Mickey packed up his drums and left. A part of me left with him that day, I felt so damn bad. He was a good guy and we had some good times. But jobs weren't plentiful and with mouths to feed, you just kept your feelings under wraps and kept on playing, until you played your own swan song for Harry.

When we finished our engagement at the Astor Roof, we were set to go back to Los Angeles to do the *Chesterfield Show*. I decided to stop off in Cleveland to see my family and pick up my wife Ruth, who had left earlier to visit her family there. I had arranged to join up with the band in Chicago, where the SuperChief stopped on its way to L.A. I went to Chicago as planned and waited, but when no one from the band had showed up by departure time, I figured I'd better get on the train in the event they had gone on earlier. Somewhere in Kansas or New Mexico, the SuperChief always passed the Chief also en route to Los Angeles. The porters on the train all knew I was with the James Band and that morning the porter in my car came by and said, "Well, there goes your band." I panicked, thinking I would be late getting to the coast, and that was not something you ever wanted to do with a guy like Harry.

As soon as the train arrived, I hopped a cab for the Gilbert Hotel, where the band always stayed. As I was checking in, I asked the desk clerk, "What rooms are the rest of the fellows in?" His eyebrows shot up and he gave me a quizzical look and answered, "What fellows? You're the only one here." Another round of panic. I couldn't figure out what was going on. Had I gotten my signals crossed? I went to bed and tossed and turned all night long, wondering if I would be employed in the morning. I had pretty well convinced myself I had really screwed up big-time!

The following morning I mustered up my courage and with a fake air of confidence went to the Lux Theater on Vine Street, where we did the broadcast of the *Chesterfield Show*. I walked in and there was Harry with a puzzled look on his face. He cocked his head to the side and, with eyes of suspicious bewilderment, said, "What are you doing here?" My heart was beating so wildly in my chest, I wasn't sure I could even speak. I turned white and red, and perhaps even blue, because I don't think I was even breathing when I bleated out, "I came from Cleveland, where's the rest of the band?" Harry proceeded to tell me that Jeep, the French horn player, had pulled the emergency cord and damn near derailed the train. This meant the band was delayed for a day and we were without a band, and a broadcast to do that afternoon. We only had Harry, who had taken an earlier train and me, who had luckily stopped in Cleveland, so Harry quickly hired two NBC staff musicians, bass and drums, to round out the rhythm section. Dick Haymes happened to be in the studio, he had just left Tommy Dorsey, so he offered to do a number with us. That was the only time the Chesterfield show ever aired without the full band. What a classic piece that would be, I wish I had a tape of that show.

Harry was a strange breed. He never showed any emotion, you never knew what he was feeling or thinking by his demeanor. The band showed up the next day and he never mentioned a word about the incident and we went on with the show as if nothing had ever happened.

During this time in L.A., we were set to do *Springtime in the Rockies* with Betty Grable, John Payne, Cesar Romero, Carmen Miranda and Charlotte Greenwood at Twentieth Century-Fox. Since we were going to be in Los Angeles for about six months, we went apartment hunting and were lucky to find a great little bungalow court apartment on Highland Avenue. Here we were right smack in the middle of the Hollywood scene, in a great apartment with two great friends from the James Band as neighbors. Shortly after we moved in, Japanese subs were sighted off Malibu. We could have picked up the entire property for twenty thousand dollars. Property on Windsor Street, which was considered very swanky, houses with swimming pools, tennis courts, maids' quarters and more, were selling for thirteen thousand. Ironic isn't it, probably today these properties are owned by Japanese. A Cadillac cost fifteen hundred dollars. I was lucky enough to have a 1934 Ford. Battered as it was, it was transportation. I still laugh out loud when I think how I used to melt rubber bands to patch tire punctures, and I can still see the guys in the band who rode with me to the studio holding up umbrellas inside the car when it rained to keep us dry.

This was in 1942, during World War II. Every man, regardless of his draft status, was issued a draft card. I was classified as 4F, because I was married and suffered from spastic colitis. We were required by federal law to carry our draft card with us at all times. Well, during all the commuting back and forth from New York and L.A., my mail never caught up with me, so my draft card was still sitting in a mail pouch somewhere between New York and L.A.

Springtime in the Rockies

During the filming of this movie, Ruth got homesick and went to Cleveland to visit her mother. One evening after shooting our segment of the film that day, I decided to take in a movie. I was driving down Hollywood Boulevard when I inadvertently made an illegal left turn. A motorcycle cop came out of nowhere and asked me for my driver's license, which I produced, and then he asked me for my draft card. My mouth went dry and my heart beat wildly as I pretended to fumble around looking for that damn draft card. When I couldn't come up the card, he asked me if I had registered. The authorities were always on the lookout for draft dodgers and here I was big as life looking as if I might be one. Even though I thought I told him very convincingly that I was not a draft dodger, he wouldn't take my word for it. He told me to follow him and as he pulled away from my car, he tossed off these words over his shoulder, "Don't try to get away." I would have sold my soul to the devil if the street had opened up and swallowed me that moment.

I followed him downtown to the police station, where I was booked, fingerprinted and questioned and in spite of my natty attire I was locked up with a bunch of smelly, dirty drunks. Here I was in my brown sharkskin suit, white shirt and tie, sitting amongst the reprobates. I was given a bunk with just rusty springs between me and my sharkskin suit to sleep on. Just before throwing me into the cell, they told me they would have to check with Washington to see if I was a fugitive from justice. There were no faxes, satellites, fiber optics or high-speed communication tools like we have today, this could take a long time. I tossed and turned all night long, frantic that no one knew where I was and here at the police station no one knew for sure who I was. I knew everyone would be concerned when I didn't show up on the set, but there was nothing I could do but wait. For sure I knew that I was scared, tired and hungry. I finally fell asleep in my natty sharkskin suit on the tangled mass of springs that passed for a bed. I had a six o'clock call at the studio the next morning, but the police didn't give a damn. To them I was just some bum who was probably a draft dodger.

The next morning "breakfast" was served. A rusty tin plate bearing a rotten ear of brown corn was handed to me. I gagged, but quickly regained enough composure to ask the guard if I could make a call. He took this opportunity to tell me that the FBI was coming in to talk to me at nine that morning; the call would have to wait. The FBI! My whole life flashed in front of me as I pictured myself on trial for war crimes, smoking my last cigarette before they tied on the blindfold and shot me. I was in a state of utter panic. What were they going to do with me, and all because I hadn't gotten my draft card, but who was going to believe me?

I guess I did have a guardian angel that day. His name was John Braun, FBI agent, and one helluva nice guy. I told him my story, and to my amazement, he said he understood. He went on to tell me that he knew I didn't belong in jail and he would have me out within the hour. As he turned to leave the interrogation room, be stopped and said, "For God's sake, Al, please carry your draft card with you at all times." I wanted to kiss his hands, but only managed to nod and weakly assured him that I would.

True to his word, I was sprung a half-hour later and on my way to the studio. Dirty and disheveled, I was beside myself with relief. What a horrible experience. I arrived at the studio just before lunch. All the guys rushed over and taking one look at me, in unison, said, "What the hell happened to you?" Now I had a reputation of being a pretty spiffy dresser and always looked fashionable. I must have been some sight that morning, unshaven, probably smelly by association and from flop sweat, wrinkled and exhausted. I told them my story, and one by one they started to laugh, until the roar sounded like the Mormon Tabernacle Chorus. They must have laughed for ten minutes. I finally joined in too. The incident was soon forgotten, but my draft card still had not caught up with me.

Harry James grooving to my beat, 1942-43

We wrapped the movie about a month later and immediately left for San Francisco and the Golden Gate Theater. One morning after finishing the performance, I was walking off the stage. In the darkness of the backstage I felt a hand on my shoulder and a voice from the blackness said, "Can I see your draft card?" I froze dead in my tracks, my mouth went dry and my heart began to pound. The figure in the shadows stepped into the light, and it was John Braun, the FBI agent who bailed me out my troubles in L.A. I took one look at him, put my wrists together and stuck them out so he could handcuff me. He shook his head and told me, "Send to Washington if you have to, but get that damn card." With that, he handed me his business card and told me to get in touch with him if I needed him. He was some special kind of fellow. I wonder whatever happened to him. As for me, the draft card finally showed up, I think after we had won the war. It's probably worth a few bucks; the head of the draft board in Cleveland was none other than Tris Speaker, the Hall of Fame baseball great. It's his signature that's on my draft card. I still have that card and guard it with my life.

After the Golden Gate engagement, Harry broke up the band. By then, my wife and I were expecting our first child, so we decided to stay in Los Angeles. I put my card in at the Union and waited for work. By the time Harry decided to reorganize the band, he called me to come back. By that time I was already doing Jack Kirkwood's show and I decided to stay put and leave the grueling one-nighters for the new kids.

Band on the Run

The bands of today travel like kings; in private jet planes and private busses outfitted with every imaginable convenience. It's a far cry from the forty one-nighters of the Big Band era.

Our bus was leased from Greyhound; it was outfitted with seats, nothing else! The men would drink and play cards, using an upturned suitcase in the aisle as a table. Bathroom duties were taken care of at gas stations, and in emergencies, sometimes at the side of the road.

The usual routine after a show was to pack up the instruments, stands, and music and load them on the bus. We would change out of our uniforms, and hang them on the bus and take off for the next city on the tour. We slept sitting upright most of the night. When we arrived at the next venue, we would use the bathroom in the back of the theater to wash up. The water was always cold, and room was always cramped, and the "bathing" was always minimal. We changed into our uniforms and often did six shows, before moving on to the next city.

We were always looking for ways to save a buck. Most of us owned a paper dickey, which we wore with our tuxedos. We would use an eraser to remove any spots, so that it always appeared to be "spotless." Close inspection would prove otherwise! But the audience never knew.

As I look back on those days, I am amazed at what we accomplished! We brought music to a world at war and joy to the people who heard us and danced to our tunes. We were paid $45 a week, and could even send money home.

The Boys in the Band

Through the decades that marked the history of the jazz and Big Band era, there are myriad of stories about crazy incidents. Musicians are wonderfully creative and funny. These are classic stories that I have never seen in print, so I will go on record with some of the crazy antics that I have been privy to.

Joe Venuti, who was probably the first and greatest jazz violinist of all time, was also known as one of the wildest pranksters in the business. He and Wingy Manone, famous New Orleans jazz trumpet player and four-letter-word man, were close friends. Wingy got his nickname because he had only one arm. He lost his arm when he was nine years old and living in New Orleans. He liked to hop on street cars and "steal a ride." The windows had grills on them, so he could hang onto them and ride free. One day he slipped and fell off, underneath the trolley car, and the wheels ran over his arm, crushing and severing his arm. He had an artificial arm made of wood. One day when he and Venuti were riding a very crowded subway in New York City, Wingy was squeezed by the crowd up against a door. At the next stop, Venuti surreptitiously put Wingy's arm in the door before it closed. Wingy couldn't feel anything, because it was his wooden arm and he was so jammed and jostled by the other passengers that he didn't notice anything going on. The train couldn't startup, as this shorted out the power.

Al Lerner

A bunch of subway workers rushed the train to inspect each car of the train and underneath it, searching for the power failure. They scurried from car to car until they reached Wingy and Joe's car, where they spotted Wingy's arm wedged in the door. Furious, they removed the arm and Wingy and threw him off the train. Joe just looked around pretending he didn't know how Wingy got his arm caught in the door.

Dick Haymes

Dick Haymes was the best damn singer of the time and the least dependable guy I ever worked with. After the James band disbanded, Dick asked me to come with him. We struck up an uneasy alliance that lasted for thirteen years. I both loved Dick as a brother and hated his behavior.

This chapter will cover my thirteen-year association with Dick, his five marriages, his eccentricities, mercurial career and life, right up to the last day of his life.

Over the years, I worked with many singers, some of whom were terrific performers and people, and some who were not. Of them all, Dick Haymes was the most complex. He could be ingratiating one moment and infuriating the next.

Dick was born in Argentina and schooled in Switzerland. His mother was a musical comedy performer who toured around the world. She always took her two sons, Dick and Bob, with her, and from time to time she deposited them in various schools throughout Europe. Dick spoke Spanish and French fluently, and had a wonderful education despite the nomadic lifestyle his mother imposed upon her children. When Dick was in his late teens his mother settled in the Los Angeles area, and Dick gravitated to the movie studios. He eventually landed little extra jobs in pictures. He can be seen diving from atop the high mast in the original *Mutiny on the Bounty* starring Clark Gable. He got that job because of his skill in diving and swimming.

Few know that Dick aspired to being a songwriter. Somehow he wangled an appointment to audition his songs for Harry James. Harry listened as Dick sang his songs. Harry, with his usual style and grace, said, "Screw the songs, Dick, come and sing with my band." I think that Dick had the best voice of all the singers. I've heard them all, from then to the present time, and Dick had something special. Unfortunately, he had so many other problems that he never reached his full potential.

We were working at the Lincoln Hotel at Forty-fifth and Eighth Avenue at this time. We were staying at the Forrest Hotel on Forty-ninth Street and across the street from the hotel was a little Greek restaurant that was a favorite hangout of the hoods in the area. One night when Dick had a date, and as usual didn't have any money, he went across the street to complain about his dilemma to anyone who would listen. One of the "boys" offered him fifty bucks on the spot, with the understanding that Dick would repay him one hundred dollars in the next week. Always foolish about money, Dick took the deal. The week passed and his "buddy" asked for the hundred bucks. Dick, of course, didn't have it. The hood told him to get it by the end of the night or he would knock Dick's teeth out. We went to work at the Lincoln Hotel that evening, and when Dick got ready to leave through the backstage entrance he saw the "boys" standing in the alley waiting for him. He ducked back into the hotel, and ran for the hotel entrance. He tried all the doors, but the boys were covering every exit. Dick knew the owner of the hotel, Maria Cramer, and he found his way to her suite. He pleaded with her to save his life. Dick turned on the charm, and Maria, like so many before and countless afterwards, bailed Dick out of his mess. I was very fond of Dick and probably understood him better than most: I forgave him all his vicissitudes.

While Dick was with the James band, he met Joanne Dru, who was a line girl at the Copa. Always impetuous, Dick married Joanne within a few weeks after a whirlwind courtship. Dick, as usual, had no money but he immediately rented an apartment on the east side of Manhattan, which even then was considered the high-rent district. The newlyweds moved into their new home with no money for furniture. They used orange crates and fruit boxes for chairs. Dick never worried about money or where his next buck would come from. Though the era of credit cards had not yet arrived, Dick usually managed to borrow enough money to stay afloat until the next job or paycheck came along.

Vamp 'Til Ready

Because Dick spoke French so fluently, almost like a native, in 1950, while working at a theater in Toronto, I came up with the idea that Dick would sing a current Tony Bennett hit in French and English at our next engagement at the Seville Theater in Montreal. The first language of Montreal is French. Dick agreed to my plan and I went downtown in Toronto to get the French lyrics for the song. I had them by the next day and presented them to Dick. He told me to hold on to them. I nudged him about the lyrics every day, and every day he told me to hold on to them. Saturday, when we only had a couple of days left before our engagement began in Montreal, I brought up the fact that I still had to write the chart. He still had to learn the lyrics in French. He snapped, "Why don't you get off my back with that song?" I quietly turned away, put the song in my back pocket, and sauntered off. I never mentioned it again. We opened Monday at the Seville in Montreal. After the first couple of numbers, people starting shouting, "Sing something in French." Dick took notice immediately and leaned down to me in the orchestra pit below. As softly as possible he asked if I had the French lyrics. I said, yes, I had them. I reached into my back pocket, held up the sheet of music with the French lyrics on it, and slowly, precisely, ripped it into shreds and let the shreds float to the floor. Dick looked stunned, though he quickly recovered and went on with the show. He pouted all the way back to the hotel, and I chose to ignore him. He knew better than to say anything to me about those damn French lyrics. Like brothers, we were soon back to normal, whatever normal was.

In 1952 Dick was booked on a tour of theaters with supporting acts such as Perry Franks and Janice, a modern dance act, and Eileen Barton, a well-known singer, who had done a radio series with Frank Sinatra. Her big hit record was "If I Knew You Were Coming I'd a Baked a Cake." Another featured attraction on the bill was The Three Stooges. Of course, they were a riot. Off stage, Moe, Shemp and Larry were very quiet and reserved, usually preferring to stay in their dressing room until time to go on. Moe was an avid reader and was an expert on trivia. They were all really nice guys, and I enjoyed working with them. During one of their numbers, they had to change their coats. So they could do this very quickly, they ran to the back of the stage where their coats were lined up in order. One day, I surreptitiously sneaked on stage and changed the order of their coats. During the act when they ran to change coats, none of them fit. The audience broke up thinking it was written into the act. I was off stage, doubled over. I thought my joke was really clever. When they finished, they came off stage looking for me. I was nowhere to be found. Ultimately, they forgave me and we remained fast friends for many years. The last time I saw Larry was at the Motion Picture Hospital after he had suffered a massive stroke. As I was leaving, he said to me, "When I get better, we're going to get the act together and go on the road." Larry died shortly after my visit. I can understand why the kids today enjoy the Three Stooges as much as we did.

We were booked into the Shea Buffalo Theater for a week. The dressing rooms were on the second floor with a concrete stairway leading to the backstage. One afternoon I dressed in my tuxedo, left the dressing room and started down the stairs to the stage, Dick was the next act up. Near the top stair, I caught my heel on the metal edge band of a stair and I slid down the rest of the stairs on my back, landing backstage. The Stooges, who were just walking off stage, gathered around me and quickly asked for someone to get the smelling salts. I was barely conscious, but could utter, "It won't help, I can't smell." While the curtain was still down the men backstage got me up and carried me on stage and put me on the piano bench and scooted me up to the piano. In a moment the curtain went up and I began to play Dick's program. I don't know how I managed to get through that show, I was hurting so badly, but I did.

When we finished the show, I was placed into a cab and taken to a nearby hospital, where they determined that I had hemorrhaged internally into the tissues of my buttocks. A large hard lump developed, which I had for many years.

After the theater tour, Dick and I went to Las Vegas to the Sands Hotel. A close friend of mine from New York City flew into Vegas to see me and catch the show. My friend, Dr. Cyril Solomon, was a cancer specialist who had written several textbooks on the subject. While waiting to go on with Dick, Cyril and I sat together at his table. I told him about the hard lump in my buttocks and that I was concerned about it, fearing it might be cancer. He suggested we go to my room and he would look at my lump. My room was quite a distance from the showroom and I knew we couldn't get there and back in time. It was almost time for our next show. Cyril said, "Let's go to the men's restroom." We left the table and headed for the men's room, where we found an attendant cleaning some shoes. The good doctor looked around and saw a closet in which the attendant kept his supplies. Cyril looked at the attendant and asked if we could use his closet for a minute. The attendant looked at him warily and nodded yes. Cyril turned and opened the door and told me to go inside. As he shut the door he said to me, "Okay, Al, pull down your pants." I did as he said, he checked my lump and told me I had nothing to worry about and it would eventually dissolve. We walked out of the closet and thanked the attendant. He was standing stock-still, eyes wide open and speechless! I'm sure he was thinking now I've seen and heard everything! I would venture a guess that he told that story more than a few times.

In June of 1953 Dick had a close friend of ours, Bob Eaton, arrange a two-week tour of Hawaii utilizing the boxing auditoriums as a venue for our live shows starring Dick Haymes. Bob's father was Cal Eaton, owner of the Olympic Auditorium, which featured boxing events every Tuesday night. Dick wanted to do this tour so that he could be close to Rita Hayworth, who was in Hawaii making the movie *Miss Sadie Thompson* with Jose Ferrer. This film was a remake of *Rain* (1928), starring Gloria Swanson.

Our first week of shows at Pearl Harbor, Schofield Barracks, and several other military installations on Oahu did very well. We featured comics who could find the humor in being in the army. The singers sang patriotic songs and ballads that reminded the boys of home. The Korean conflict had been raging in Asia, so we did what we could to bring a little cheer to the kids who were so young on their way to war. The first Sunday we had off, I was invited to lunch at Rita's apartment. Joe Ferrer was there. We all sat around and talked and had a few drinks. Soon the conversation turned to tennis. Ferrer asked Dick if he would like to play that afternoon. Dick declined, but said that I could play. Joe asked me and I accepted. About an hour later we met at the Royal Hawaiian Hotel, where Ferrer was quartered. We warmed up a bit and started to play. I played high-level tennis at home almost every day since moving the California in 1942. Immodest as it may be, I was and still am a pretty fair tennis player. I beat him quite handily, not realizing that he was taking this all very seriously. Rather grumpily, he said, "I'll play you tomorrow when I haven't been drinking." I responded with, "I will not have been drinking either." We reserved a court for the next morning. The next day I arrived at the appointed time and proceeded to beat him more soundly than I had the day before full of booze. He stormed off the court without even shaking my hand.

Years later, Rosemary Clooney, who was a good friend of Ruth and me, called and during their conversation Ruth invited Rosie for dinner. Rosemary had been married to Jose Ferrer, but was now divorced from him. They, however, remained friends and good parents to their five children. Rosie asked if she could bring a friend. My wife said, "Of course."

That evening I answered the doorbell to find Rosemary standing there with Joe. He looked at me rather sheepishly, and came in. We had a lovely dinner and lots of good conversation. Needless to say, the subject of tennis never came up. I appreciated Joe's taste in pianists. He was a huge fan of my mentor and friend, Art Tatum. What the hell, I thought; he can't be all bad if he likes Tatum.

As we completed our first week, Rita finished shooting the film. When she left for Los Angeles the next day, Dick left with her. The acts in our show and I were unaware of this event and we were shocked to find out we were left holding the bag, so to speak. Chaos and panic reigned among the members of the show; fortunately, we all had return tickets to get back home. No one had been paid at this point. The comic had no money and became so depressed that he committed suicide in Hawaii.

Hawaii was not a state in 1953, so everyone was required to have the necessary valid documents to reenter the mainland. Dick was not a U.S. citizen; he had been born in Argentina. This was just the opportunity that Harry Cohn, president of Columbia Pictures, was hoping for. Harry had a personnel vendetta against Dick. He wanted Dick out of Rita Hayworth's life. She was Harry's most prized possession and a moneymaker for his studio. Stories of Cohn's ruthlessness abound;

it was well known to everyone in the industry that Harry didn't let anything stand in his way. Harry alerted Immigration that Dick was returning to the United States. The Immigration Service held Dick, and it made the front pages of every newspaper across the country, though eventually they had to let him in.

Shortly after returning home I received a call from Louella Parsons, asking me what I knew about all that had transpired that lead to Dick's detainment by Immigration. She went to say, "After all, you and Dick have been so close for so many years, you can probably tell me something." I wasn't about to give them anything that might be damaging to Dick or to Rita. There were a lot of rumors around Hollywood that Dick had been set up, but like everything in show business, it wasn't front page for very long and the rumor died. Of course, Harry's plot to get Dick away from Rita didn't work. They were married in September 1953.

It was common knowledge in the industry that Harry Cohn was the most feared and hated producer in films. Cohn was so disliked that after seeing the huge crowd at his funeral, a reporter remarked, "If you give the people what they want, they'll turn out for it."

In September of 1953 we were appearing at the Sands in Vegas when Dick received a call from Glen McCarthy, owner of the Shamrock Hotel in Houston. Dick owed him a date and Glen told him, "I want you in October." After we completed the Sands date, I told Dick that I was through, that I would not, could not continue as his musical director. Dick was in dire financial straits and hadn't paid me my salary for sixteen weeks. I was falling behind in my bills and worried how I would keep my family afloat. I said my goodbyes in Vegas and drove home to Studio City and my family. I was both sad and relieved to finally break free from Dick, the financial uncertainty and his destructive and manipulative behavior.

Just before Dick was to open in Houston, he called me and pleaded with me to go to Houston just for the opening night to rehearse the show. Honeymooners Dick and Rita wanted everything to be perfect. After mulling it over, I agreed to fly down for the opening, but emphasized that I would leave the following day. I rehearsed the show and that evening we did it to a full house. While Dick wowed the audience, most everyone kept looking at gorgeous Rita. After the show Dick and Rita cornered me and said, "You're already here, so why don't you stay for the full engagement? We'll set the wheels in motion to get the back pay owed to you." I agreed to stay on those terms. Do I need to add that I never got any money at all? Again, I had let myself be conned.

Dick and Rita were fighting all the time. Late one afternoon, the three of us were having a drink in the Cork Club, a private pub within the hotel. While we sat at a booth, Dick and Rita got into it over some trivial matter. I got up when the fighting started and went to the bar. After a few minutes I heard some screaming, and looked back to see Rita on the floor pulling and scratching at Dick's face. The hotel's security officers came in and quickly got both of them out of there and up to their suite. I was embarrassed and kicked myself for getting into this rotten situation another time.

At the close of the engagement Saturday night I caught the "red eye" to Los Angeles. Dick asked me to take the music library home with me. He was contracted to open in Pittsburgh at the club called the Carousel, owned by Little Jackie Heller, a well-known performer of the thirties. Dick was heavily promoted, and Heller was hoping to cash in on the fact that Rita would be ringside every evening.

I had finally had it with Dick and all his shenanigans. I had no intention of going to Pittsburgh. Early Sunday morning I got a call from Dick's agent. He asked me to open with Dick Monday. I told him I would if David Marcus, Dick's attorney, would guarantee that I would get my money. He replied, "I can't do that." I said, "Then I don't go."

Later that morning I got a call from Hal Howard, vice president of M.C.A, Dick's booking agents. Hal opened with, "I understand you're not going to open with Dick in Pittsburgh tomorrow. What kind of shit are you pulling?" I told him I couldn't possibly go, as I didn't have any money. Dick hadn't paid me for sixteen weeks. "Whoa," he said, "what do you mean you haven't been paid?" I told him the whole story. Astonished, he said, "We haven't received our commission in months because he told us he had to square his account with you." In closing he said to me, "You're not going to Pittsburgh and, don't worry, we'll keep you busy." Shortly after, Howard was killed in the crash of a private plane headed to Vegas to a Sinatra opening.

Vamp 'Til Ready

I advised Dick's attorney that I would bring the music library to the airport and ship it cargo so it would be there for Dick's rehearsal at the Carousel. The attorney told me there would be a plane ticket for me at the counter if I changed my mind about going to Pittsburgh. Not this time. I wasn't going anywhere except back home and to work for someone who paid me.

Monday morning, I picked up the *Los Angeles Times*, and, behold, on the front page: "Dick Haymes in New York Hospital." The article said Dick had checked in with an undisclosed condition and would be staying for observation. So typical of him! This ploy meant he wouldn't be able to open at Little Jackie Heller's club and, furthermore, he wouldn't be in breech of his contract. If a performer is hospitalized, it is covered by the "Act of God" clause in most contracts. Dick destroyed Little Jackie Heller's Carousel Club with his "condition," which was nothing more that his own self-serving mentality.

Several years later I was working with Frankie Laine at the Concord Hotel in the Catskills. On the afternoon of our first show, a group of hardliners from the other hotels in the area came over for cocktails in the lounge to welcome Frankie to the "Borscht Belt." We all introduced ourselves to each another. I was sitting directly across the table from a gentleman I neither knew nor recognized. I said, "I'm Al Lerner." His eyes widened and he said, "I'm Jackie Heller." He looked at me with a menacing gaze and blurted out, "Al Lerner, you son-of-a-bitch, you ruined me." He went on to accuse me of being responsible for his Carousel Club folding. I stood up and said, "Hold it, hear my side of the story before you pass judgment on me." I related chapter and verse of the incident that resulted in the closing of his club. Jackie listened intently, shaking his head, and then he apologized. For many years after Jackie and I enjoyed a friendship.

A few months later I was working with Frankie Laine in New York. We had a date to open an engagement at Lou Walters' Latin Quarter. (Lou, incidentally, was Barbara Walters' father). I had heard that Dick was now living and working out of New York, and I had a garage full of Dick Haymes' musical arrangements that I had stored at my home for years. They were all original scores from Dick's recordings and movies written by Victor Young, Gordon Jenkins, Sonny Burke, and even some by me. I phoned M.C.A., Dick's booking agents, and got his phone number in New York. I called him that afternoon for the sole purpose of telling him that I would send him a carton of his music. He was very happy to hear from me, although I was suing him for my unpaid salary. Dick's first comment was, "Just because I owe you this money, what's that got to do with you and me?" He asked if I was available that evening to have dinner with him and his lady friend at their apartment on the east side. I said, "Ah, what the hell, why not?"

I took a cab over to the east side and stopped off to get a box of candy for his live-in friend. Dick greeted me as if nothing bad had ever happened between us. His lady brought in some drinks for us, but most of the time she stayed in the kitchen preparing dinner. Dick and I drank and reminisced about all the things we had done during our years together.

At some point, between swigs, Dick asked if I would like to hear his newest album, which was about to be released. "Of course," I said. We were pretty bombed by this time. Dick played a few tracks and then asked me how I liked it. I replied slowly and warily, "Do you really want to know?" Dick said that he did, and I blurted out, "I think that it stinks, that isn't you." He became furious and loud. Kitty, his lady, had heard our conversation and came into the living room and said to Dick, "You've always said how much you respect Al's judgment, so listen to what he has to say." Dick jumped up and lunged at her and got quite nasty. I stood up and grabbed him. He swung at me and I returned the blow. By then we were both on the floor punching wildly at each other, knocking over a lamp and upending an end table. We finally quit, exhausted and feeling pretty stupid. Dick glared at me and said, "Get your coat and get the hell out." I said, "Okay, but she goes with me." I was afraid he would take his anger out on Kitty, so she got her coat and we left together. I know we went to a bar on Forty-ninth Street called the Spindletop, where they knew me. And that's all I remember!

The next morning I awoke in my own apartment with dried blood all over my face, shirt and undershirt. I tried to remember all that had happened the night before, but I drew a complete blank. I phoned my wife in Los Angeles and told her the whole story and admitted how

Vamp 'Til Ready

embarrassed and disgusted I was. Ruth, who never got excited about anything, calmly and reassuringly told me that everything would work out fine.

When I hung up the phone, it rang again. I picked it up and the voice at the other end shyly said, "Hello, Al, this is Dick. What the hell happened last night?" After we both apologized, Dick said, "What are you doing tonight?" I replied, "What are you selling this week?" Dick asked me to come back and promised there would be no booze. I went over that night, rang the bell, and Kitty answered the door wearing an apron like nothing had ever happened.

I didn't see or hear from Dick for long time after that, but eventually I began to hear rumors of his being ill. I didn't know how seriously then.

Then one day Dick called me and asked if I would come over and visit with him. I was stunned to see my old friend, dying of lung cancer, looking old, sick, and tired. I put on my best face throughout our visit. He asked me if I would come back again and bring a tape recorder. The following week I returned. I recorded a ninety-minute story beginning with how we met and continued to the present. Not too long after that Dick went back to the hospital. I called Nora Eddington, Dick's third wife, with whom I had remained close even after they broke up. I asked her if she would like to go to Cedars to visit Dick as I had a strong feeling that this would be our last opportunity to see him before he died. I picked her up and headed for the hospital. When we got to his room, the curtain was drawn, covering the doorway. There were doctors on both sides of his bed administering treatment. We waited in the hall until they finished and then went in. Dick grabbed me and looked up into my face and made a few barely audible sounds. Nora and I tried to make him understand that he should rest while we sat quietly at his bedside. Nora and I said our goodbyes and left my old friend. Shortly after returning home, the phone rang, and it was Cedars telling me that Dick had expired. I was relieved and grateful that he wouldn't have to suffer anymore, but I was overwhelmed with sadness; Dick had been a big part of my life.

None of this is meant to be derogatory, but merely truthful. Dick could be a very giving person. I understood his shortcomings, which emanated from his childhood years and lack of early parental guidance. For the most part of our thirteen-year relationship, Dick and I got along well and had many great experiences; we were like brothers.

THE WAR YEARS

Dick Haymes and I were rejected from military service. He was classified 4F because of extremely poor eyesight. I don't know why I was excused, but I was told it was because of a spastic colitis condition. Instead of fighting the axis in some foreign land, Dick and I entertained injured soldiers in military hospitals. These were occasions I will never forget. It is easy to forget the power of music when you're the person who is busy making the sounds. We would enter the wards to see row upon row of hospital beds filled with young men. Most of them were lying quietly, and when they looked at you, their eyes would break your heart. Then, we would start, and when the music filled the room, you sensed an awakening, almost a relief to be taken out of their personal reveries. We played our hearts out. I was never able to leave any of the hospitals without crying; a tear from each soldier.

When I wasn't busy with Dick, I would go with two wonderful girl singers, Helen Forrest, whom I worked with in the Harry James Band, and Liltin' Martha Tilton, who became popular with the Benny Goodman Band. She was most famous for her great rendition of "And the Angels Sing," along with Ziggy Elman, the great trumpet player and composer of the song.

Helen and I did many shows for returning wounded veterans in Navy and Army hospitals. An upright piano would be pushed into the wards on a wheeled platform, so the soldiers could see us. Helen would walk around each bed and sing the songs she made popular: "I Don't Want to Walk Without You," "I Had the Craziest Dream," "I Cried for You," and more. The boys just loved her, and she loved them.

One young man in the ward was a Navy pilot who had been shot through the eye and was blinded during the flight. His wing mates talked him down to a safe landing back to his aircraft carrier. What an amazing story of heroism.

You never saw such an outpouring of appreciation; you would think we had done something wonderful, when, in fact, those kids deserved our appreciation and love. As was usual for me, I would cry when I left, and so would Helen.

Helen, Dick and I did a show in a camp in North Carolina. The commanding officer graciously offered to fly us to New York, where we were opening at the Roxy Theater the next day. We boarded a small six-seater and took off for New York City. As we neared our destination, the pilot asked the co-pilot for the map so we could land at Floyd Bennett Field on Long Island. The co-pilot turned to the pilot and said, "I thought you had the map." Gulp, no one had the map. To compound this dilemma, it was getting foggy and overcast. My mind was racing with thoughts of hitting one of the skyscrapers that dotted the landscape of Manhattan. Dick, who was a pilot, appeared nonchalant about the situation. My palms were sweaty and I wondered if I would ever see my family again. My fears were soon allayed when I heard the pilot radio the tower. The pilot got us down safely. The ground never looked so good.

When we completed our engagement at the Roxy, I decided to return to California by train. I had quite enough flying for a while. I wanted my feet on the ground, or rails as the case might be. One afternoon, between shows, I walked down to Penn Station to purchase my ticket. As I was walking down Madison Avenue, past the Empire State Building, a piece of metal fell to the sidewalk in front of me, then a tire bounced onto the street. I looked up, but did not realize what I had just witnessed. Some people ran out of the building, yelling that a plane had just hit the Empire State Building. I ran to Penn Station. That settled it. I *wasn't* flying home!

After the war ended, Martha Tilton and I were invited to entertain for Air Force Day in Merced, California. Marshall Thompson, who later became known for his television series, *Daktari*, Martha and I, boarded an Army C47, which was to take us to Merced.

Vamp 'Til Ready

Martha Tilton sent me this just before she died

Fliers were coming in from all parts of the country for this great celebration. We were about thirty minutes out of Merced when, out of the clear blue, two jet fighters dived out of the sky, seemingly from nowhere. It felt like we were going to be attacked. We watched, petrified, as they pulled up alongside our plane, using their flaps to slow enough to be able to cruise alongside our plane. It got even scarier when they began to tap the end of our wings with their wings. Again, my heart was racing, my palms were sweaty, and I thought I was gong to die.

Martha, always a trouper, got out of her seat and went forward into the cockpit, and asked the pilot to get them on the radio. He complied. Cool and collected, Martha told them in no uncertain terms to stop endangering our plane and theirs. She promised to meet them at the bar when we landed if they would go away and leave us to complete our flight. They complied, and Martha returned to her seat. She said she suspected that they had already been to the bar, because of their wild laughter when she talked to them. Martha married a test pilot, so it takes a lot to shake her up; she understood planes and pilots.

I breathed a sigh of relief as we touched down in Merced. As we suspected, the jet pilots were waiting for us, and they were indeed drunk. Though it wasn't funny, we humored them; after all, we still had to return home by plane.

We were introduced to the big brass at lunch. Martha was crowned Queen of Air Force Day, and was asked to ride in a convertible during the parade down the main street. I rode behind her in the next car with Marshall Thompson. As we started down the street, a jet fighter suddenly loomed in the distance. He leveled off and, right over our heads, he buzzed down the street. At the end of the street, he pulled up sharply. The crowd gasped collectively in horror, as they saw his auxiliary wing tank fly off and land in the parking lot of the local hospital. I don't know what happened to the pilot, but my guess is that he was busted out of the air force.

Martha has gone to Australia with me, doing the Benny Goodman segment of our show. She is a wonderful singer, and a great person. Martha and I have remained friends throughout our lives. Sadly, now we usually only see each other at funerals of our friends and fellow performers.

Glen McCarthy

In the 1960s I conducted several shows at the Shamrock Hotel in Houston, Texas. The owner, Glen McCarthy, was a larger-than-life personality known for his wildcatting in oil. Hugely successful, this magnificent hotel was a glowing testament to his good fortune. The movie *Giant*, with Rock Hudson, Elizabeth Taylor and James Dean, was the loosely disguised story of his life.

Glen had asked me to move to Houston and take over the job of Musical Director of the hotel. I did and was ensconced in a lovely suite with a piano. It was during my tenure there that I heard many of the legendary stories about him.

During construction, Glen needed a lot of money to cover expenses. He went to his insurance company to float a loan. They turned him down. Not one to forget, he filed this away in his brain under personal insults. A few years after the hotel was completed, the same insurance company booked their convention there. One evening, the CEO, who had turned Glen down for the loan, booked a reservation in the hotel dining room. The entourage in their white formal attire was seated at their table and had already ordered the first course when Glen came into the dining room. Glen called their waiter over to his table and whispered instructions to him. Shortly after, the waiter entered the room carrying a tray of gazpacho. When he went past the CEO, he pretended to trip, spilling the soup all over the white coat of the CEO. The waiter immediately apologized and attempted to wipe the soup off the white jacket. The CEO took off the jacket and hung it on the back of his chair. As soon as he did this, the Maitre d' came to the table and asked him to leave the restaurant. The policy was coat and tie only. No exceptions.

Al Lerner

Dick Haymes was appearing at the hotel six nights a week. On his day off, Glen invited Dick and his then-wife, Nora Eddington, and me to drive to Galveston. He wanted to take us to a well-known watering spot at the end of the pier, The Balinese Room, for a drink or two. We spent an uneventful couple of hours there and then the four of us piled into Glen's big Cadillac for the ride back to Houston. En route, Glen stopped at another bar. As we walked into the place, Glen strode over to the bar, grabbed a pretty young woman sitting at the bar and kissed her. When her date got off the bar stool and came toward Glen, Glen threw a punch and the young man ended up on the floor. We all turned and walked, quickly, out! We jumped into Glen's car and sped off into the night. Within a few minutes a cop car, with the siren wailing, the light shining at us, pulled up behind us. The policeman took a look at the license plate, and apparently recognized who was in the car, made a one-eighty, and split. I guess that's when you know "you've made it."

Hadacol Caravan

In 1950, while I was still working with Dick Haymes, we were offered a tour for a couple of weeks. The tour's sponsor was a new product called Hadacol. Hadacol was an elixir ballyhooed as a cure-all for aches and pains. Senator Dudley LeBlanc of Louisiana and Colonel Tom Parker, Elvis Presley's manager and partner, were proponents of this product. They had shills on the train who would attest to Hadacol's amazing effects. I recall one lady stating to the rapt crowd that she could sit on a stone-cold floor and get up by herself without any discomfort. It was wildly popular, until the government regulators discovered it had 18-percent alcohol content. It was quickly pulled from the shelves of pharmacies, but not before Senator LeBlanc and Colonel Parker had made a tidy sum of money from sales.

The tour was first class! Called the "Hadacol Caravan," the show had its own private train. While in towns along the tour, the train pulled onto a siding, it functioned as a hotel. There were many well-known movie and radio stars, and each week the lineup changed when a new group of entertainers came aboard. While Dick and I were on the bill, we also had Carmen Miranda, Bob Hope, Mickey Rooney, Rochester, Jack Dempsey and a line of dancing girls. Also with us were Hank Williams and his band and a group of animals who were used in the parade held in each town touting the show. Ted Evans, nine feet, four inches tall, billed as the tallest man in the world had an act that included a midget. The train with its star-studded cast wended its way through the Bible belt. The price of admission was two box tops from Hadacol, and because we drew such large crowds, the shows were held in stadiums or ballparks.

Al Lerner

My fighting buddy, Jack Dempsy, around 1950

With Ted Evans, the 9'4" tallest man in the world

Vamp 'Til Ready

We even had a doctor on board who set up a mobile infirmary on one of the train's compartments.

In every town a beauty contest was held and the local winner would join the show. At the end of the tour there was to be a final contest with a big prize for the winner. The girls were chosen and screened by the henchmen of the CEOs for their willingness to participate fully. At one point in our tour, Senator LeBlanc was summoned to New Orleans on a political matter. I guess he wasn't about to leave all those young beauties with the motley crew of henchmen. He issued an order, "Get rid of the girls." That night the train pulled up to a platform in some remote town and the girls filed out of the train, left to find their way back to their hometowns. I don't even know if the girls were given any financial compensation. We never saw the Senator again; he threw in the towel with the tour and our show. I don't know if he was reelected either. I hope not.

Carmen Miranda had her contingent of Brazilians backing her in her act. She was a doll to be with, but had one outstanding problem. Carmen was a hypochondriac of the first degree. All you had to say to Carmen was "You seem pale," and she would panic. Cleverly, she carried her own doctor in the show, who happened to function as her guitarist as well. Everyone behind the scenes and out front loved Carmen.

Jack Dempsey, the great heavyweight world champion, did his bit on the show. He told the story of the long count legendary to his title fight with Gene Tunney. I was and still am a huge fan of the fights and an admirer of Jack Dempsey. I hung around with Jack a lot and we became fast friends. He was a great kidder and so was I. We were constantly pulling pranks on each other. One day our train was on a siding in Macon, Georgia. I was outside playing catch with one of the guys in the show. I had my shirt off; Dempsey came off the train and playfully grabbed me on my bare chest. The other fellow had a camera and shot of a couple of pictures. At our next stop he had the pictures developed. Standing alongside the train, I showed the photos to Jack and laughingly said, "I'm going to send these pictures to one of the tabloids and show the whole world you're a sissy." I had enough sense to start running away from Jack at that point. Jack took off after me and chased me around the train. He never caught me and I sneaked back onto the train and hid out in a friend's compartment.

Jack Dempsy and me

The following morning while eating breakfast in the dining car, the door opened and in strode Jack. He immediately spotted me, came over to my table and said, "Hello, kid." Playfully, he threw a punch at me, which nearly knocked me through the wall of the train. With a twinkle in his eye, he said, "Aw, I didn't mean to hurt you, kid!" He sat and ate his breakfast as we pulled into Cincinnati, Ohio.

The owner of a local roller rink boarded the train and issued an invitation to the entire cast and crew to come to his rink after every show. He wanted to keep the rink open for us because Jack Dempsey was his sports idol.

That evening after our show, Dick Haymes, Nora Eddington (Dick's wife), Carmen Miranda, her husband David Sebastian, Jack Dempsey and I went to the roller rink to skate. The owner was so thrilled to have Jack there that he kept everyone on the staff there after hours, from the organist to the person who helped you put on skates. Jokingly, we all stepped onto the rink and tentatively everyone began to skate, except me. I surveyed the situation, because I was an expert skater as a kid, and knew I would still skate rings around everyone there. I spotted Jack clumsily pulling himself around the rink by hugging the railings and the walls. I had decided this would be the perfect place to get even with Jack of punching me in the dining car. I circled him, showing off my agility on skates. I skated backwards, inches from his face, and said, "Now we're even, you're in my arena of expertise!" I proceeded to punch him and scoot away. "I'll kill you," he said. I shouted back over my shoulder, "You'll have to catch me first." I twirled around doing my best pirouette on skates, and laughed. He tried to chase me down, but he was no match for me that evening. We finally called a truce and sat down to take off our skates. We started laughing so hard, that we laughed all the way back to the train. Jack and I remained close friends for the rest of his life.

The Hadacol Caravan finally wound up in Dallas, Texas. The top dogs sponsoring this unusual show had left the tour, and signaled that this was the end of the line. We were to find out just what kind of people had put this entire package together. The circus animals were left for the taking by anyone who wanted to take them. The most crushing blow of all was when none of us got paid. Everyone had to find their own way home. I was under contract to Dick Haymes then, so I wasn't part of the litigation, but I don't think any of the performers got what was due them.

Jack Dempsey and I spoke on the phone often, but I didn't actually see him for about five more years. I was on my way to Salt Lake City via Western Airlines. I was meeting up with Frankie Laine there for a concert appearance. As I sat waiting in the terminal, I was started to hear a familiar voice say, "Hey, Kid." I jumped up to greet Jack. He was very excited to tell me he was on his was to Las Vegas to show his friends around. He had been in Los Angeles because the night before he was the surprised guest of Ralph Edwards' show, *This is Your Life*. He then grabbed me around the shoulders and marched me over to meet his friends, Luis Firpo and Georges Carpentier! To a boxing freak like me this was ringside heaven. My mouth fell open and I could hardly say hello I was so thrilled to be in the company of three of the greatest boxers of that era. They had made boxing history. As luck would have it we were all on the same plane, I had a stop in Las Vegas. Even if I hadn't, I think I would have changed by ticket just for the chance to talk to the three of them together.

The four of us settled into a section of the plane that had a table between the seats, and began our flight. We started talking about their lives and boxing. I was fairly conversant in boxing, my dad had fought professionally under the name of "Kid Tucker," and I had boxed some as a kid. Luis Firpo just sat and watched. He didn't speak a word of English. I recall, Jack looked out the window of the airplane and pointed out little towns where he had boxed in his early years. He told me about the referees who had tipped him off during a fight. His opponent was getting tired and it was suggested to him that he should work on his body. Jack also told me that he would, in a clinch, bite his opponents on the muscle of their shoulder, which would practically paralyze their arm. He went on to tell us that these fights only paid him ten dollars and he would take pretty bad beatings. He couldn't afford to hire someone to care for him, so he stayed at a house of prostitution where the whores would tend to his wounds and nurse him back to health.

During the flight, Carpentier left to use the men's room. Jack used this opportunity to extol the great ability of Georges. Later when Jack left, Carpentier leaned over me and whispered, "Boy, could he punch." I was so thrilled to be in the presence of these three great fighters, but I was even more impressed with the mutual respect they had for each other.

We landed in Las Vegas and got off the plane to be greeted by a swarm of photographers. They were waiting to take photos of these great champions. I, like a jerk, stepped aside. In retrospect I wish I had stayed put and been in the picture too. I often think back over that special flight, and I still get goosebumps.

After that evening, I didn't see Jack for about three years. I was in New York City working with Jimmie Rodgers at Silverman's on

Broadway, just a couple of blocks from Jack Dempsey's Restaurant. On the afternoon of our opening, I went by Jack's place and looked in the front window. Jack spied me and waved me in. His first words to me were, "Have you eaten, kid?" I guess he thought I was in New York broke and hungry? I assured him that all was well and that I was in fact opening that evening with Jimmie Rodgers in Silverman's just down the street.

We opened that night to a sold out crowd. After the show, Jimmie and I went to the lounge where there was a radio host, like so many clubs of that era. The purpose of the host was to interview people who came in to see the show. Visitors to New York were thrilled to be on the radio. Out of the corner of my eye, who did I spot, but my old buddy Jack Dempsey coming down the stairs carrying a huge strawberry cheesecake from his restaurant. His restaurant was famous for this dessert. He gifted me with the cake and I shared with everyone there. What a great guy! I never saw Jack after that, and shortly thereafter he died. I was so saddened by the passing of this great champion and my special friend.

Howard Hughes

Rumors have it that Howard Hughes would phone for a cab to meet him at the fire escape of the Desert Inn Hotel when he was going out for the evening. I was working at the Sands Hotel with Dick Haymes in September of 1953. One night between shows, I was sitting in the lounge with my old friend, Dorothy Collins, star of *Your Hit Parade*, and the Sands entertainment manager's secretary, Eleanor.

Eleanor saw Howard and called him by name, motioning him to come to the table. The name Howard meant absolutely nothing to me until she introduced us, Howard, Al Lerner, Al, meet Howard Hughes. I almost fell off my chair. Here he was unshaven, wearing a white shirt and slacks, looking like a mess. Very shortly, it became very obvious that he had "eyes" for Dorothy.

After our second show, Dorothy, Myron Cohen, a wonderful comic with our show, and I went to the Frontier Hotel and over to the crap table with Howard in pursuit. Myron Cohen took out a roll of bills and put a hundred dollars on the line. Howard Hughes arched his eyebrows in utter amazement. Howard had only bet a silver dollar. When Howard turned to me to tell me Myron had bet a hundred dollars, I couldn't believe my ears, this coming from one of the richest men in America.

We left to go to the El Rancho; Howard was not in our party, but followed us there. Every time we looked around, he would jump back behind one of the pillars he was hiding behind in the casino. This went on until almost six in the morning. When all the stories began circulating about Howard's strange behavior, I was not in the least surprised. I had witnessed it up close and personal.

Frankie Laine

Frank and I first met in Cleveland, where we were both working little joints which all had little trios or quartets. Most of them had backup singers or dancers to entertain the guests. Frank was originally from Chicago and migrated to Cleveland. He, like I, worked for almost nothing. It was amazing how we could get along on fifteen bucks a week. I'm sure when Frank worked he didn't make any more than I did. He finally got a job at a place called Parker Appliance. Now he could draw a salary every week.

I lost track of him after I left Cleveland to join Harry James in New York City. The next time I saw Frank was in Hollywood in 1945. He drove up to my apartment with the idea of writing songs together. It didn't work out for me as I was doing a five-day-a-week radio show, *The Jack Kirkwood Show*. The next thing I knew Frank was working on Vine Street at a club called Billy Berg's.

A leading disk jockey allowed Frank to record a couple of numbers on someone else's recording session. This was possible because there was about twenty minutes left on the allotted three-hour session. Well, need I tell you? The rest is history.

I followed Frank's career through the papers and air play, but seldom saw him. In 1954 I was playing tennis at the home of Frank Cooper, a radio producer who lived in Royal Oaks in the San Fernando Valley. During one of our games, I head someone from the adjoining house call to me. It was Patty Andrews of the Andrews Sisters. I walked over to the fence and said hi. She said, "You'll probably be getting a call from Frankie Laine." I asked, "Why me?" She told me that Carl Fischer, Frank's pianist and conductor, had passed away the day before. I was very saddened to hear of Carl's passing. He was a very nice guy and

Al Lerner

good pianist. In fact, he and Frank wrote "We'll Be Together Again," which is a beautiful song and a standard even to this day.

I dismissed Patty's remark, thinking it was just an unfounded rumor. However, when I got home, my wife said that Milt Krasny, who was Vice President of G.A.C. (General Artists Corporation), called and had asked me to return his call. I called Milt, who asked me if I would be interested in going with Frank. I asked Milt what cities would be on his forthcoming tour. Milt told me that he would next go to Chicago and a few other cities, then on to Europe, culminating the tour with a Command Performance for Queen Elizabeth of England on November 1, 1954. I asked Milt to wait a moment. I put my hand over the mouthpiece and asked my wife if she wanted to go to Europe to see the Queen. I got a wildly enthusiastic nod. I then told Milt, "We've got a deal."

I went without Ruth on the first leg of the tour, which was solely in the United States. During that time I learned a great deal about Frank. He was probably the most relaxed and calm individual I had ever worked with. I must relate a story which I think illustrates what I mean by that.

We were appearing at the Chicago Theater and a fellow came to the stage entrance and wanted to show Frank a song he had written. He, of course, hoped Frank would like it enough to record it. As was my practice with all the singers with whom I've worked, I screened all the people who made those types of requests and evaluated their validity. This fellow had a small portable record player and a dub of his song. Talk about being prepared. I checked with Frank and he offered to see him.

As the fellow walked into the dressing room he asked, "Frank, are you Italian? I'm Italian too. I got kids, and, you know, if you make a record, the kids could get some money."

Frank said, "Let's hear the song."

The song was, and I am being generous, very amateurish and unprofessional.

Frank said to him, "Let me play you a song that Mitch Miller turned down, and this was written by a well-known writer. Do you think your song is as good as this one?"

Joe Louis, Frankie Laine and I, around 1955

The would-be songwriter, incredible as it seems, then said, "Frank, you and me we're Italian, I got a couple of kids. You put my song on a record …. well, you know what I mean."

Frank sat very quietly for what seemed to be a very long time. He looked intently into the man's eyes and said, "If one of your kids had appendicitis would you let me operate on him?"

The man's eyes opened wide, his nose wrinkled and he said, "Frank, you ain't no doctor."

Frank replied, "That's right, and you're not a songwriter and I won't put my life in your hands either." Frank had a lot of style when it came to handling people and I admired that about him.

The European tour and Command Performance were both exciting and very successful. I will never forget the night of the Command Performance. My wife and I were getting dressed to go to Albert Hall. She stood in the middle of the floor, twirling in her beautiful ballgown and said, "Imagine, little Ruthie Levokovitz from Sutton, West Virginia, going to see the Queen of England." It was a thrilling experience and one I won't ever forget.

Frank had literally thousands of adoring fans. He was always gracious and accommodating to every one of them. While in London we had an incident that again shows Frank's ability to deal with difficult situations with amazing grace.

Frank and I had worked out a plan when we entered the theater. This plan was necessary because Frank's fans were lined up hoping to catch a glimpse of him or touch him and even grab a piece of his clothing. Our plan was that whenever we left our car, I would closely follow Frank so that no one could come between us. In this way, I could protect him from someone coming up from behind and surprising him.

A Rolls-Royce and driver were at our service to pick us up from the hotel and drive us to the London Palladium, where the performance was to be held. As we drove up to the backstage entrance, a very large crowd had gathered hoping to catch a glimpse of the stars that would be appearing that evening. Our driver opened the door and Frank stepped out to a blaze of home camera flashbulbs and the usual screaming. I immediately followed him out of the car, but a fan had somehow managed to wedge herself between the two of us. She reached up and grabbed his hair hoping to get a lock of it as a souvenir. Frank, like many artists, liked to augment his hair with a small additional hairpiece, because it was thought to look better on stage. The fan gasped as she looked into her hand only to find she had pulled Frank's hairpiece right off his head and down his back. The astonished fan, in her shock, dropped the toupee onto the sidewalk. Without skipping a beat, Frank spun around and said, "Now aren't you ashamed of yourself?" With that, he scooped up the toupee and we proceeded into the theater, where Frank replaced his hairpiece. He was really amazing.

Sunday is the day off at the London Palladium so Frank and I decided to go out to dinner. Frank called his manager, Cres Courtney, and said he had a great idea for dinner. We would go to each restaurant that was famous for a specialty and we would have just that one course and move onto the next restaurant. It would like a progressive dinner. Our first restaurant was famous for an appetizer, which we had and left for our next course. We went to another restaurant for a fish course. We went to Simpson's for roast beef. By this time we were pretty full, but Frank said we had to have dessert. Frank had read about a Greek restaurant in Soho renowned for its baked apple dessert. We took a cab, which left us off in an alley, which happened to be where the restaurant was located. What we didn't know was that it was not open for business on Sunday. As we turned from the doorway, we were confronted by five "Teddy Boys." Teddy Boys were the English equivalent of American Zoot Suiters.

The boys were probably seventeen or eighteen. There were five of them and three of us. We were considerably older, and I don't mind telling you we were a little uneasy in this deserted alley, with no one else in sight. We were all thinking we were probably going to have to fight our way out of this one. Frank spoke up first and said we were going to go to this restaurant but didn't know it was closed on Sunday. The boys seemed a little surprised and one of them said, "Eh, they're American!" Cres seized the moment and said, "This is Frankie Laine." Another one of the kids gave him a sideways glance and said, "Come on." Fortunately, one of the other boys said, "Yeah, that's him, that's Frankie Laine." This seemed to diffuse the situation immediately and we all relaxed. In fact, the kids wanted to escort us out of there, as this wasn't a proper place for Frankie Laine to be, of all people.

When we finally found a cab, Frank asked the boys if they would like to come to the Palladium to see the show. He told them to go to the stage door on Monday. He would be expecting them. Too bad, but the kids never did show up, probably thought Frank really didn't mean it. Frank never made idle promises. The kids would have had wonderful seats for the show and the time of their young lives.

In February of 1955 we left for Australia. In those days of prop planes, it took thirty-six hours and four stops to complete the trip. Our third stop was Fiji. We had a mechanical problem with the aircraft, so we had to stay over on the island to wait for a new part. Meanwhile, we were put up at the Mocambo Hotel in Nandi! Rather an exotic name for such a small hotel. We were introduced to a Scottish fellow who was born on Fiji to Scottish parents who had immigrated there. He was employed by the hotel and was assigned to show us around the island.

Al Lerner

He was, in fact, Colonel in charge of the Fijian Army during World War II. Bet you didn't know Fiji had an army!

He escorted us to a native village with grass huts like we used to see in *National Geographic*. He took our group to the hut of the chief of the village. We had to stoop to enter the hut, which was quite large. In the middle of the room was a long table, with cups and a bowl of ominous-looking liquid in it. We were invited to sit, and cups of a native drink called Kava were ladled into cups fashioned from coconut shells. Our guide told us to take the cup in both hands and to drink the liquid down and to please act like we were enjoying ourselves. I looked down into the cup in my hands and saw a thin, whitish-looking concoction. I like to try new things and I have an adventurous nature. I put the cup up to my lips and drank it down, as instructed. My eyes widened and I mustered every bit of bravado I possessed and bravely smiled. Kava is a horrible-tasting liquid, somewhat like fermented Kaopectate. Immediately, my cup was refilled. Now I was really in a bind, it would have been horribly rude and unthinkable to do anything but to pretend you were enjoying the drink; trust me, I wasn't enjoying this drink. It was all I could do not to gag, so I persevered, and every time I smiled, my cup was refilled. I must have passed muster, because they finally stopped passing out the liquid. I should have been given an Oscar for that performance. To this day, thin, milky-looking substances make me queasy.

The chief sat on his chair and watched us carefully. He was a large and quite impressive man. A large necklace of whales' teeth hung around his neck, a display of his rank and his importance. He appeared to be puzzled about who we were and why we had been brought to his village to meet him. Our guide spoke to him in Fijian, apparently to explain who we were and why we had come to Fiji. As they spoke to each other, I glanced around the hut and I noticed a small radio. I wondered what they could possibly listen to way out here in the middle of the Pacific Ocean. I was soon to find out. We listened to what sounded very strange to our ears, when in the midst of all this unfamiliar talk, we heard our guide say "Frankie Laine." The chief's eyes widened and he sat forward and let out a howl – "OOH, 'Mule Train.'" We didn't know whether to laugh or cry in relief. Here we were in a remote part of the

South Pacific and the chief knew Frankie Laine and "Mule Train." The chief's body shook with laugher, relieved, we all started to laugh. In spite of the liquid beginning, we had a very enjoyable afternoon with the chief and the villagers. Fijians are very warm and hospitable people and made us feel very special indeed. It was a memorable afternoon. To this day, I don't smile if I don't like something I am drinking or eating.

After the necessary repairs were completed on our Pan-Am Clipper, we left for Sydney, Australia, our final destination. We were to perform at the Sydney Stadium, which was a fight venue. Many great fighters had gone the distance in this stadium, one of whom was my close friend, Jack Dempsey.

Lee Gordon was an entrepreneur from Detroit, Michigan. Before 1954, very few American performers came to Australia because they couldn't get paid in American dollars and the exchange rate was not

Al Lerner

favorable to performers. Lee Gordon had many connections in Las Vegas, and with his Vegas compadres, worked out a system so entertainers could get paid in American money. The Australians would give the performers vouchers, which they could take to Las Vegas and exchange for their salary, which would be converted to US currency. This opened the door for American stars that were wildly popular in Australia to come "down under."

By 1956 Lee Gordon had experienced a few setbacks. One of the biggest was when Frank Sinatra didn't appear for a scheduled date. He started his long descent down into drugs, and was found walking the streets. It was a long way down for this clever man, who had once had this part of the world by the tail.

Nat "King" Cole, who was one of the nicest men I have ever had the privilege to know, came to Australia for a date booked by another promoter. When he heard what happened to Lee Gordon, he felt so sorry for him that he gave two plane tickets to Lee and his wife to go anywhere in the world. They settled in Europe, where Lee died. It was the end of a wonderful era in Australian musical history.

We opened to fantastic crowds, doing two and three shows a day. One Saturday night after our last show, Lee Gordon had set up a dinner party at Milano, an Italian restaurant. The restaurant was already closed for the evening, but had been contracted for a special party honoring Frank. We were seated with friends, eating antipasto and sipping our cocktails when the owner came over to the table. We were introduced all around, and then Mr. Milano looked directly at Frank and asked him, "You like Italian food?" Frank casually replied, "Yes, I'm Italian." Milano said, "Laine, that's not an Italian name. Frank replied, "That's not my real name; my name is LoVecchio." Milano paused, looked at Frank quizzically, and said, "Where you from?" Frank said, "I'm from Chicago." Milano went on to say, "Your mother and father, they still alive?" Frank responded that they indeed were still alive. "Is your father's name John?" asked Milano. Frank nodded yes and looked at me, as if to say what the hell is this all about? Milano went on, "John the Barber?" Frank leaned forward in his chair trying to figure out where this was all going and said yes. Milano ran to the side of the table where Frank was sitting, threw his arms around Frank and started to

Vamp 'Til Ready

sob. Through his tears and sobs, he blurted out that he and Frank's father had come from a small town of Monreal in Sicily together to America. Mr. Milano opened a little produce stand next to LoVecchio's Barbershop. Indeed, Frank's father was known as "John the Barber, and was, in fact, Al Capone's personal barber. Halfway around the world a connection was made that lead all the way back to Sicily. It is truly a small world after all.

We went on to Brisbane to complete the tour. Eileen Barton and I decided to take a walk one afternoon and take in the town. We spotted a bakery and decided a spot of tea and pastry would hit the spot. We stood in front of the pastry case and looked at all the tasty things to eat. We made our selection and I walked over to the register to pay the tab. We noticed a sign behind the cashier that read "Casket Closing Today." We asked the clerk, "Can we get in the casket before it closes." The clerk replied of course. I guess we were the ugly Americans that day, as we burst out laughing and couldn't stop. When we finally regained some composure, I asked the clerk what that meant. In Australia they have a lottery, and the tickets are pulled from a wooden box, ie., casket. Though we made complete fools of ourselves that day, I still chuckle when I think about how the very same language can have such different meanings.

I have gone down under often afterward, doing shows at the Sydney Opera House and other large venues all over Australia for a total of twenty-seven times. During one visit I was offered house conductor of the biggest and best hotel in Tasmania. After a lot of deliberation, I felt I couldn't move my wife, children and mother so far away from the family. So I refused. Often I have often wondered what my life would have been like if I had taken the job. I have always had a very special place in my heart for Australia and the people. I still am in contact with the many close and dear friends I made there over the years. They come to see us and every year I promise myself, "one more time." Maybe this year.

During one of our trips to the continent, we were playing in Rome when we were asked to one of the big Saturday night specials. This one was being held in Via Reggio. Via Reggio is probably best known as the marble capital of the world. It is not too far from the Leaning Tower of Pisa. We arrived by train late in the afternoon and went immediately to rehearsal. I had a fairly difficult time communicating with the musicians, none of them spoke English, and my Italian is practically nonexistent. Somehow we got through the music for the show that evening, using a combination of my pidgin Italian, body language, sign language, and most importantly the understanding good musicians have of the printed word. Music really has no language barriers. The show was scheduled for nine o'clock, so while we were waiting, our hosts gave us some wine and food. It was just minutes before nine and I had not seen the director since rehearsal. There were few musicians scattered around and I began to worry. The theater was filled and the audience was seated, waiting for the performance to begin. I finally found the stage manager, and pointed to my watch, which now read ten after nine. He just shrugged, and said something that roughly translated into "somewhere around nine." I began to feel panicky. I had never run into this before. Nine-thirty the director of the band finally showed up, and, if by magic, so did the rest of the band. We assembled on stage and the show began. In spite of the late start, the show went off without a hitch. Frank was a huge success, as always. The Italians loved their native son.

When the show was finished, we were taken back to the train station to return to Rome. Frank and I had been eating our way through Italy. We were feeling a bit bloated and out of shape after a week of feasting. In those days, I could eat pasta and Italian cuisine like it was the last supper. We decided we were going to go on a diet and just order fresh salads and fish dishes. It was about midnight when we got back to the train station. We walked into the train station and there we smelled the most delectable aromas emanating from an all-night restaurant. Resolute in our dieting plans, Frank and I ordered a salad which we intended to split between us. While waiting for the salad, we looked at the tables around us. There were platters of antipasto, fettuccine, chicken, veal, savory-looking dishes everywhere. We were surrounded by a veritable feast. We divided up our salad and lackadaisically began to dig in. After a few bits, of what was really a very tasty dish, Frank put down his fork, looked across the table at me and said, "Who are we kidding?" Frank called over the waiter and pointed to the table next to ours and indicated to the waiter to bring the same to our table. Platter after platter came out of the kitchen, steamy strands of spaghetti, dressed with a fresh tomato basil sauce, succulent chicken cacciatore and a creamy risotto. We ate and ate, and when we finished, we could barely push away from the table. Our all night train to Rome arrived and we boarded. We hurried to our respective compartments. Almost before I said goodnight to Frank and shut the door, I grabbed my belt and began to get out of my pants; the waistband had become so tight, I could hardly breathe. I sat down on the edge of the bed, unzipped my pants and breathed a sign of relief; my belly was as big as I had ever seen it. I couldn't see my feet. Now I knew how my wife felt when she was nine months pregnant. I leaned over to untie my shoes, and found out that I couldn't bend from the middle; this meant I couldn't reach my shoes. Frantic, I tried to bring my leg up and reach over my belly. Nothing I tried worked. In a sweat, I lay back on the pillow and felt like crying. My overindulgence had really wreaked havoc! I was forced to sleep with my pants down around my ankles all night, until we finally arrived in Rome the next morning. I felt no better that morning, but knew I had to do something pretty quickly, or I felt like I would explode. I even considered checking into a hospital to get my stomach pumped. I pulled my pants back up, leaving the button undone, and belted on the last notch and disembarked. Standing in the sunlight, I came to my senses and decided to walk off the previous evening's meal. Briskly, I walked and walked until I couldn't take another step. After about two hours, I went to the hotel, entered my room and fell onto the bed, exhausted, and fell into a deep sleep. About five o'clock, the phone rang, and it was Frank. He told me that we were meeting Mario Lanza in the bar. I got up, showered and dressed very quickly. I felt pretty good. I looked at myself in the mirror and saw that my belly was almost back to normal. I promised myself right then and there that I would order more wisely at the restaurants in Italy.

Mario was in Rome making the movie, *Seven Hills of Rome*. It didn't take long for me to forget my personal promise. We had a couple of drinks and then went into the restaurant for dinner. Antipastos, pasta, chicken, veal and more were laid in front of us. All my good intentions flew away the moment I took in the aroma; my stomach ruled again and I dug in.

Our next encounter with Mario was in Las Vegas. Frank was appearing at the Desert Inn and Mario was opening across the street at the Frontier Hotel. On the day of Mario's opening, the House sent up a case of champagne to his suite. As the story went, Mario was "scared stiff" about appearing live, which wasn't his forte. He commenced drinking the champagne until he was bombed. He passed out on the bed in his room. Show time, no Mario! There was a full house, and the audience was getting restless. When it became obvious that Mario would not do his show, the Frontier called the Desert Inn and asked if Frank and I could quickly, and I do mean quickly, come across the street and do the first show. We bundled up the music, dashed across the street and Frank filled for Mario Lanza.

Billy Daniels, of "That Old Black Magic" fame, subbed for him on the second show. The story that buzzed through the grapevine the next day was that the hotel had advanced him fifty-thousand dollars; that was a lot of money in the fifties. The people who ran Las Vegas then didn't tolerate behavior like this. He was put on a train and sent home the next morning. Mario never appeared in Las Vegas again. I never saw Mario again, but did spend an evening with his mother. Mario had died in 1959 and his mother was still mourning his passing. She told me that she didn't think Mario had died of a heart attack as reported. He was only thirty-eight.

Frank and I had traveled to Rome for a concert. We had just finished our first half and were backstage chatting with some guests. There was a rather attractive young woman in the group and we began talking. She had asked me where we had been in Italy and the places we played. I asked her if she would like to have something to eat and coffee with me after the show. We completed the second half of the show and again gathered backstage with our guests.

I changed out of my tuxedo and came out to meet her. We hailed a cab, and as we were riding through the streets of Rome, it dawned on me that she spoke English. Curious, I asked her where she learned to speak English so well.

She replied, "I've been to America."

I asked what had brought her to the United States. She went on to say that she went to visit her sister. I asked her where her sister lived, and she responded "California." At this point, I was beginning to wonder if I knew her sister, there was something very familiar about this young woman. She told me her sister was an actress.

"Who is your sister?" I asked.

She turned slightly, looking straight at me with big brown eyes and said, "Sophia Loren."

Of course, I was flabbergasted. She spoke to the driver in Italian and soon we pulled up in front of an apartment. We walked up a flight of stairs, she opened the door and we walked in. A tall, very striking woman came to greet me. I knew instantly she was Sophia's mother. The resemblance was remarkable. Mrs. Loren made some coffee and fixed some food. We sat down and talked. Sophia's sister interpreted for me and we laughed and I had a thoroughly enjoyable evening. My hosts were gracious, and both very beautiful. That time with the Loren family was as good as meeting Sophia; the evening will always be very special to me. I left and returned to my hotel. I learned later that Sophia's sister married Mussolini's son, who was a jazz pianist in Italy.

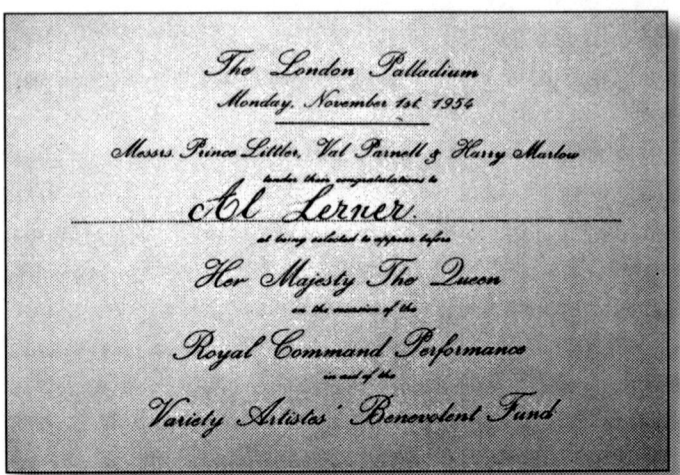

BUDDY RICH

In 1956 Frankie Laine put together a show in Sydney and Melbourne, Australia for the Olympics. Participating with Frankie in the show was singer Eileen Barton; Joe "Fingers" Carr, Ragtime Pianist; Buddy Rich, one of the greatest drummers ever to grace a stage; and the wonderful comic, Stan Freberg. We were sold out.

Joe "Fingers" Carr had a very unique act. He would cover the piano keys with a very sheer strip of silk, put on gloves and place black silk blindfold across his eyes. He would then play the best ragtime piano imaginable. Buddy Rich was on the bill just before Joe. This night, Buddy came on stage, covered his drums with a cloth, put on gloves and put on blindfold. He then beat out pieces on the drums while the audience went wild. We all stood in the wings aghast, utterly disbelieving what he was doing. Joe yelled out, "What the hell is he doing to me? He's ruined my show." At that moment we all knew that we were involved in a hell of a dilemma, one that was not going to go away. This began the shunning of Buddy. Buddy truly became "persona non grata"; everyone stopped speaking to him.

After we closed in Sydney, we had a one-day show in Newcastle. Everyone in our little troupe went by bus, with the exception of Buddy. Instead, he borrowed a car from an Australian comic, and drove the 75 miles to the gig. After the show, which went off without incident, we all went back to Sydney by bus, Buddy by car. Two days later the comic called me and asked where his car was. I had to tell him that I didn't know; after all, I wasn't speaking to Buddy. He finally located Buddy, who told him that he had run out of gas and left it somewhere on the side of the road between Newcastle and Sydney. This gave new meaning the expression "Ugly American."

We were asked to do a benefit show in Sydney Town Hall, starring Stanley Holloway. You will remember him for "Get Me to the Church on Time" from *My Fair Lady*, both the stage and film productions. Once again, Buddy came on just before Stanley. He was introduced, and out he came, tap dancing and singing "Get Me to the Church on Time," Holloway's featured number. Stanley stood in the wings as we watched him turn pale and gasp in utter disbelief, "What's he doing to me?"

That was the crowning blow.

We left Australia and went on to Manila to do more shows there, no one speaking to Buddy. We arrived on schedule, and took cabs to the hotel, all arriving at the same time. We were standing in front of the hotel, when Buddy's wife and daughter got out of their cab and waited for Buddy to pay the driver. Apparently, the taxi driver did not see that Buddy had his arm on the door post when he shut the door on Buddy's hand. He screamed and fell to the ground. We all remained standing on the sidewalk; no one made a move toward him. The hotel called for an ambulance and took him to a hospital. He returned sometime later with his hand all bandaged. No one seemed to care. The pro that he was, Buddy went on that night and played with one hand. Buddy could play his style of music on the drums with one hand better than most can with two. He was an amazing artist.

What a shame when a person is imbued with so much talent, and Buddy had tons of it, that he behaved so badly that he alienated every one of his peers. He was probably the greatest drummer of the time. He could do things on the skins that no one else could even imagine doing. He was truly one of a kind. It's so easy to be gracious, kind, generous, and grateful to be able to bring your special talent to so many. He never understood that concept.

AL MARTINO

I received a call at home in California from Al Marino. He asked me if I would be interested in joining him as Musical Director and Pianist. I was always interested in new accounts, so I agreed. He was currently appearing at the Coconut Grove in the Ambassador Hotel in Los Angeles.

Al had a front table reserved for me to watch and critique his performance, which I did. Afterward, I joined him in his suite to discuss the notes I had taken during the show. He liked what I had to say and the changes I would like to see in his selection of songs. He agreed with most of them and we seemed to get along well. After we discussed our business arrangements, we talked about our forthcoming tour in Australia.

I wrote some new arrangements for him and shortly thereafter we left for "Down Under." At the Los Angeles Airport we picked up our tickets, which had been forwarded by the producers of his show in Australia. The clerk handed Al the tickets. One was first class and the other was economy, for me, of course. Al turned to the ticket clerk, and said, "My conductor flies first class with me." He pulled out his wallet and paid the difference in price! After some of the cheapskates I had worked with, I was really impressed, a very decent guy.

Upon landing in Melbourne we were greeted by the Media. This involved several interviews. This was a first for Al, but I had already been there many times before, so I guided him through the whole process.

A limo was waiting to take us to the hotel where we would be appearing. En route we drove down a street where a new building was under construction. Al asked the driver to stop when he saw a group of bricklayers at work. Al got out of the limo, walked over to the workmen and asked for a trowel and some bricks and mortar. They stared at him in amazement as he quickly and very deftly laid a course of bricks in a matter of moments. They were astonished. When he stopped he told the men, "After all, I come from a family of builders, I learned to lay bricks as a kid." Some photos were taken that day, and ended up in the Melbourne papers the next day. Good publicity! He shook hands all around and jumped back into the limo, and we drove away.

The show went off without a hitch to very enthusiastic audiences. He liked to introduce me and tell the patrons that I had been to Australia so many times, that the first time I came was with Captain Cook. It always got a laugh.

Al found a good Italian restaurant and he ate there every night! He used to like to say, "These are my people." The same dish every night too, calamari. After the show on our last night in Melbourne, the owners of the Italian restaurant invited us there for a going away party. I had a prior invitation, so Al went alone. When the meal was over and it was time for him to go, the owners came over and handed Al the tab for the party. On the plane home I ribbed him all the way, "So those are your people."

We had a few more dates, but most of his engagements were on the East Coast, I needed to stay closer to home. So we parted friends. I always think fondly of him when I think of the good time we had working together. I hear him on the radio often and he sounds better than ever. Good going, Al.

Rudy Vallee

Rudy Vallee was one of the leading stars of radio in the thirties and early forties. He headlined a top show of the period, *The Fleischmann Yeast Hour*. The theme song was "Your Time Is My Time," which, of course, he sang every show.

At his hilltop home in Hollywood, when you rang the doorbell it played his theme song. As you entered the living room, you were taken aback by a huge floor-to-ceiling picture of a knight in armor with the visor open. Need I tell you whose face adorned this abomination — none other than Rudy himself. Placed as conspicuously as possible, was a large plaque engraved with "The Vagabond Lover."

Rudy told me that he purchased the home on top of Mulholland Drive from film star and leading lady Ann Harding. The property was a magnificent two-story home with a view of Los Angeles that was magnificent. One of the most unusual aspects of the home was the driveway. There wasn't sufficient room to turn a car around once you reached the front entrance, so the architect built in an electric turntable that turned your car around for you. Can you imagine?

There was a beautiful tennis court and theater below the "castle." The theater could seat more than one hundred. This palatial estate could not have been complete without the shrine to Rudy. This was his "museum," as he liked to call it. There, he displayed all his records, music, pictures, and various artifacts.

I was invited every weekend to his home to play tennis with him. Most people were not aware that in the entertainment field, Rudy was the "King" of frugality. Cheap says it even better. I can't remember that he ever offered me a drink, or asked me to stay for refreshments. He was so stingy, that he even had a very special brush custom made to bring up the nap on his tennis balls. He never opened a can of balls! I would constantly try to get out of these tennis games, but he would even send a car for me, if I told him my car was in the shop.

During this time I had a trio and played at the Century Plaza Hotel in Beverly Hills. The hotel was quite new and the "in" place to be seen. One of tables at the other end of the dining room was particularly enthusiastic in their applause. When we finished the set, I walked over to the table to thank them. I immediately recognized by their accents that they were from Australia. When I told them how many times I have traveled there to work, they asked me to sit down and join them. The gentleman at the head of the table introduced himself to me; imagine my surprise when I found out that I was speaking to none other than the Prime Minister of Australia, Sir Robert Askins. During the course of our conversation, I spoke of my close friends, Ken Rosewald, Frank Sedgeman and Lew Hoad, Australians who were top tennis players of that time. In passing, I mentioned that I played tennis with Rudy Vallee that morning. Sir Robert stopped me cold and said, "*The* Rudy Vallee?" I said, yes, and he asked me if I could possibly arrange for him to meet Rudy. It seems that Rudy was his idol, which I thought might be a joke, but he was dead serious. I told him I would arrange it and asked him to phone me to confirm it.

The next morning, he called. I said to Sir Robert, "I thought you were kidding!"

He replied "No, I want to meet him."

I told him I would call Rudy and would get back to him.

I called Rudy and told what had transpired. He said he would send his driver to the hotel to pick up the Prime Minister and his party and bring them back to his house for drinks. After that he would take them all to Lawry's Prime Rib for dinner. This was and is a well-known Steak House in Los Angeles that always comped Rudy and his guests. Don't think for a moment that Rudy was going to pick up the tab! Rudy called me the next morning to tell what a great time they all had, and that they would be leaving for Hawaii the next day and then back to Australia.

A few weeks later I received a letter from the Prime Minister with a copy of the Sydney newspaper with a front page story by the Prime

Minister thanking me for getting him together with Rudy Vallee, plus a note saying that if I came to Australia again he would be happy to do anything for me. I will never forget Sir Robert.

I continued playing tennis at Rudy's home for some time. One day he told me about a vitamin he was taking that would enable him to live forever. He died shortly after that conversation while lying in his bed watching television.

George Gobel

The greater part of my active musical career has been spent with top vocalists and the Big Bands. One of the rare exceptions was with a very lovable and talented, one of a kind, down home, funny man, George Gobel. There was never a sweeter or nicer fellow in show business. What most people didn't know was that he was probably the shyest man in the business.

When I first met George, he was appearing at the Coconut Grove at the Ambassador Hotel on Wilshire Boulevard. This was the place to go if you wanted to see movie stars and celebrities. It was their favorite watering hole. Every night of the week the room was filled with luminaries and the top talent of the day was the headliner in any given week. It was the place to be and be seen.

George called me and asked if I would come to his suite before his show. He said he would like to discuss some aspects of his forthcoming tour. I, of course, went down to the hotel to meet with George.

We talked for a while, and then he asked me if I was wearing a watch. "Yes," I said, wondering what he meant by the question. "May I borrow it?" asked George. I unbuckled my wristwatch band and handed over the watch to him. "Now you'll have to stay to see the show if you want to get your watch back," he said, all the while grinning from ear to ear.

What else was I to do but stay and watch the show (pun intended)? It would have been bad form for me not to, even without the watch trick. As usual, George, who was unique and very talented, gave a wonderful show full of clever dialogue delivered as only he could do it. When he was through, we went back to his suite. Shortly after, Bobby Byrnes from MCA came to the suite.

Al Lerner

Looking over arrangements with Geoge Gobel

Bobby was formerly the road manager for Tommy Dorsey during the days of Sinatra, The Pied Pipers and Jo Stafford. Bobby was also an old friend of mine going back to my days with the bands. What most people never knew was that George didn't drive a car, and Bobby had come to take him home. We had a couple of drinks and chatted a while, when suddenly George said to Bobby, "You can go home if you want to, Al will drive me home."

George changed out of his tuxedo and we left the hotel for our respective homes in the San Fernando Valley. I maneuvered my car out of the hotel garage and drove onto Wilshire Boulevard. George sat quietly for a couple of miles, intently watching my every move. Suddenly, he blurted out, "You're a great driver; you drive right between all those white lines."

We arrived in Encino where George lived, and he told me to go to a bar and grill on Ventura Boulevard. As soon as we walked through the door, I realized that George was a regular there; half the room greeted him with "Hey, George." He seemed to know everyone. We had a few rounds of drinks when George said to me, "Why don't you mosey over to the piano and play something, I feel like singing." I obliged and George asked me to play a World War I song, "My Buddy." George sang and the room fell silent, you could have heard a pin drop. He sang it so sweetly and so poignantly that I got the impression some of the people in the bar thought he had lost someone in the war. The song is naturally a tearjerker, and George did it justice that evening.

When he finished, a well-dressed couple came up to George and told him what huge fans they were of him. George took the opportunity to invite them back to his home for a nightcap. We left the bar, drove to George's house with the couple following us. George opened the front door, walked over to the staircase, and yelled up the stairwell, "Spooky Ol' Alice, come on down."

In a few minutes Alice appeared, dressed in her robe and started to pour drinks for everyone. After we finished yet another drink, Alice went into the kitchen to make some scrambled eggs. We ate, and rather abruptly, George turned to the couple and said, "Good Night!" They got the message and took their leave. By then I had lost count of how many drinks we had downed, and I thought I'd better get home. I asked George for my watch and was flabbergasted to see that it was four o'clock in the morning. "George," I said, "my wife is going to have a fit."

I departed and wove my way home, relieved to pull into my driveway. Apparently, Ruth heard my car, and jumped out of bed and headed for the door. The door swung open, and I saw Ruth crouched on the floor. "What the hell are you doing?" I asked incredulously. Ruth looked at me with fiery eyes and yelled, "I tripped over the telephone cord in the bedroom when I got out of bed and I think I've broken my toe." Broken it was and her toe had to be placed into a tiny cast. Ruth's disposition was just great; she never held any grudges nor got angry. Soon we were laughing about the whole incident.

A few weeks later we embarked on the Midwestern tour. I was contacted by George's agent in Los Angeles and asked if I was interested and available to play for and handle the musical part of a tour though the Midwest. George was already a favorite of mine, so I considered working with him a privilege more than a job.

We got together and conceived a show consisting of several musical and humorous tidbits. The opening act was a country-style trio called the Traveler's Three. We rehearsed only a few times, and those times were quite enjoyable.

The tour was to start in Minnesota, so we all met at the Western Airline terminal to board the Champaign flight, just about four o'clock in the afternoon. The bass player of the trio wouldn't check his instrument, so George bought a round-trip ticket for the string bass.

George and I settled into our seats, with the string bass comfortably ensconced in the aisle seat across from us, and started the first leg of our tour. Shortly after takeoff, the stewardess came down the aisle and asked us what we would like to drink. I ordered a Vodka Martini, and George mumbled, "The same." A few minutes later our martinis arrived with the ever-present peanuts and were placed on our tray tables in front of our seats. I deemed it appropriate to toast our new relationship, so with a flourish I raised my glass and said, "Here's to a successful tour, George." I took a short swig, looked over my glass at George, who was staring at me. I was taken aback. "Do you know what you just did?" George asked somewhat ominously. I looked at him quizzically and thought, Holy Christ, did I blow it already? I replied, "No, I don't know what I did." With that George turned in his seat and summoned the stewardess, and when she asked if she could be of help, George asked her to put a "head" on my drink. She filled my glass once again to the brim. Feeling rather unsure about this whole situation, I thought, what the hell? I raised my glass and said, "Here's to a successful tour" once again and this time took a long pull on my drink. George slapped his knee, stared at me, and said, "You did it again," this time in a rather loud tone of voice. I'd had it. I blurted out, "I did what again?" In a slow and deliberate manner, George said, "You drank from the rim of your glass and you never spilled a drop." He then picked up his glass, with a trembling hand, and splattered some of his drink onto his trousers. Curiously, he slid his glass over to me, and without any words, indicated he wanted me to drink the head off his glass. I obliged, not knowing that from that moment on, I would officially be in charge of drinking the head off all of George's drinks so he could manage them without spilling. I might add I got a little bombed from time to time because of this nightly ritual. There was a two-drink rule on these flights but George wasn't through drinking. He called the stewardess over and said, "I paid for the seat with the bass in it, so I want the bass's drinks." He got them.

The last stop on our Midwestern tour was a date at the Municipal Auditorium in Dayton, Ohio. The show was scheduled for Mother's Day, which was also the official opening of a season. The doors had been closed all winter long. After we arrived at the auditorium and deposited our wardrobe in our dressing rooms, George and I walked out front and he peeked out through the drawn curtains to check out the house. The capacity of the auditorium was about twenty-five-hundred, so imagine George's dismay when he saw only two hundred or so people scattered about the theater like fly shit. Visibly shaken and disappointed, George shuffled back to the dressing room. George was a proud man, and I knew he would give this performance his all, just as if it were standing room only.

Al Lerner

In concert with George Gobel in Dayton, Ohio

I wandered around backstage and spotted an old twisted tennis racquet. The strings were broken, the frame twisted, the mangled mass hanging bleakly on a nail. Underneath this sad sight, was a small hand-printed sign reading "Bat Bat!" Being an ardent tennis player myself, I was curious and perplexed. When I saw the stage manager, I walked over to him and asked to explain the meaning of the sign. In a surly tone, he replied, "Just what it says." When he saw my confused look, he explained that since the auditorium was closed all winter, bats came in and settled into the beams and rafters. When the doors reopened in the spring, the bats, attracted to the stage lights, would swoop down over the stage and the auditorium. I nodded in disbelief and walked away.

Meanwhile, back in the dressing room, George, depressed, had opened a bottle of scotch and had a few belts trying to bolster his mood before going on. The show opened with the Traveler's Three, and then George Gobel was introduced. They wheeled the grand piano onto the stage; I sat down and played the familiar tune that was his trademark entrance music. George sauntered out onto the stage and went directly into his monologue. He tailored his act for this audience, telling them about his turbulent plane ride to Ohio.

Suddenly, out of nowhere, two bats were flapping in and out of the spotlight. George stopped dead for a moment, recovered, and started again. I had never heard him falter during his monologue before, so I was somewhat surprised. Slowly and deliberately, George started over again, when whoosh, a few more bats flew through the rays of the spotlights. George, with a look of utter panic, turned to me and shouted, "Play me off!" I obliged, the curtain came down and I left the stage to see what had happened to George. I found him sitting at his dressing table with his head on his folded arms. He had an aura of total despair. I stopped in front of him and said, "How about those bats?" He jumped up and shrieked, "You saw them too?" He was elated, and there stood in front of me a new George, exuberant, restored, and relieved to find out that he wasn't having DT's or seeing apparitions on stage that afternoon. He picked up his glass, poured himself a drink, held it up, and said, "Same game!"

Al Lerner

With George around 1972

Joan Crawford

During the sixties I was doing a lot of freelance conducting and accompanying various recording artists and motion picture performers for G.A.C., William Morris, and M.C.A. Bobby Byrnes, a vice president at M.C.A., frequently called on me to act as musical director for one or another of their stars. I got a call from him one day asking me if I would be a guest at Joan Crawford's sixteenth birthday party for her daughter Christina. I was to go to her party not only as a guest, but I was to be available to play for any of her guests who might get the urge to sing. He stressed that I should consider myself one of Miss Crawford's guests.

I arrived at her Brentwood home, and Joan answered the door, carrying a huge brandy snifter of liquor. I introduced myself, and she said, "Come on in, let's have a drink together."

The celebrities in attendance included Jeff Chandler and Jane Wyman. Jane had married a good friend of mine, Freddie Karger of Columbia Pictures, years after she dumped the future president of the United States, Ronnie Reagan. Everybody who was anybody in Hollywood was there that day.

The party was held on the back lawn, there was plenty of food and booze, and Joan had an upright piano strategically placed just in case someone decided to sing. As the day wore on, because of Brentwood's proximity to the beach, the air became damp and chilly.

Jane Wyman began singing outside, but soon grew uncomfortable in the cool, damp air. "Al, come in the house. There's a grand piano in there and I feel like singing some more." I was only too glad to comply. The piano keys have become wet and slick and I was pretty cold. Jane and I went inside to the piano, and she sat down on the bench beside me while I played her favorite tunes and she sang. After about fifteen minutes, a very drunk Joan Crawford strode into the room, those big brown eyes of steel glaring down at us, and said to Jane, "What the hell is going on in here?"

"We were cold," said Jane.

I said nothing.

"Do you think you're too damn good for the other guests?" Joan demanded.

Jane attempted to explain, and said quietly, "No, Joan, I just wanted to sing a few songs with Al."

They argued back and forth, and Joan blurted out something nasty to Jane that I couldn't hear. Jane apparently had enough. She stood up and punched Joan right in the face...kaboom!...Joan fell to the floor. She screamed at the top of her lungs, calling Jane every unsavory name imaginable before she ran upstairs to her bedroom.

The party fell apart rather rapidly after that with guests scurrying out of the yard and into their cars. The only two left were me, because I didn't know what to do at that point, and Milt Racmil, president of Universal Pictures. He and I had just decided that we would leave too when Joan came staggering down the stairs. Here was the Queen of Hollywood looking like something out of Sunset Boulevard: mascara running down her face, lipstick smeared, hair flying in every direction, clutching a drink. Weaving her way into the living room, she nonchalantly asked me if I had anything to eat, had I had enough food? The conversation went downhill from there; one inane question after another. It didn't take a genius to figure out that she was pretty drunk. I finally took my leave as gracefully as I could; after all, I didn't want to screw up for Bobby Byrnes. MCA gave me a lot of jobs and I had a lot of mouths to feed. Somehow I came out okay with both Crawford and MCA.

Years later, I was conducting shows in Hawaii for Kay Starr, who was a close friend of Jane Wyman's. Jane flew over to catch Kay's performance at the Kahala Hilton before going on to Maui. During the day we all hung out around the lagoon at the hotel. I had a funny feeling that even though Jane was very friendly, she just couldn't remember where she knew me from.

One afternoon, Kay, Jane, and I were sitting around a table in Kay's bungalow, when I looked straight at Jane and said, "I have two words for you, Jane!"

"What are they?" she responded.

"Joan Crawford," I said.

With that, Jane jumped up, threw her hands up in the air, and then, pointing a very long finger at me, said, "It was you!"

We must have laughed for an hour as we recounted that wild, wacky afternoon at Joan Crawford's party.

JIMMY DOOLITTLE

As a young boy in 1930 I was fascinated by airplanes and fliers of World War I. I read all the magazines, but *Battle Aces* was my favorite. My imagination would take me to the skies, where I would fight imaginary air battles with the fictional pilots.

Cleveland, my hometown, was the venue for many air races. The most famous and certainly most exciting one of that era was the Thompson Trophy Race. The course was set out like a speedway, only in the air, with pylons that the pilots had to race around. To enter the event, a minimum speed:. To enter the race, a minimum speed of two-hundred miles per hour had to be recorded in your name. These pioneers of aviation loved the thrill of flying and would nearly scrape the ground with their wings to give the audience thrills and chills. The greatest names in flying of that time were entered this day, most notably, Roscoe Turner and Major Jimmy Doolittle.

Roscoe Turner was some flier, but what made his daring feats even more amazing, was that he always flew with a full-grown lion in the other seat. It was quite a sight to see the lion staring straight ahead, as if he was the copilot, his mane streaming in the wind behind him. Roscoe had been given the lion when he was just a cub, the lion, not Roscoe. He raised his lion and they became inseparable. When Roscoe and his lion deplaned, the lion would walk next to Roscoe, untethered. The lion was apparently oblivious to everyone except Roscoe, but the people nearby scattered like startled zebra on the savanna. That probably wasn't necessary as the lion paid no mind to anyone or anything except Roscoe and their plane. I heard that Roscoe eventually had to give the lion to a zoo, where he visited his dear pet every day for the rest of its life.

Al Lerner

Amelia Earhart was participating one day, flying an autogyro, a forerunner of the helicopter. She was sponsored by Champion Sparkplugs. She was engaged in a sham battle with another well-known pilot who was flying a 1914 "Pusher." This is a plane with an exposed cockpit, the pilot sitting on a platform with the prop behind him. I watched in horror as one of Amelia's blades caught his craft in a close encounter maneuver. He plunged to the ground and was killed instantly. You never knew what you were going to see at the races.

I got into the races under the guise of selling ice cream bars. I would pick up my box of bars from the vendor and fly as fast as my feet would carry me onto the field. I was supposed to work the stands and sell the ice cream. When I hit the tarmac, I dumped the ice cream and stood transfixed at the side of the field taking in the glorious sights and sounds of the aircraft. This day, Jimmy Doolittle was scheduled to fly his Gee Bee Sportster. It was single low-wing craft with the cockpit placed right in front of the tail. To enter and exit this airplane one had to crawl through the fuselage to the tail. Jimmy took to the air and began to race around the pylons, as fast as he and his plane could go. On one pass over the field, his engine burst into flames. He maneuvered the plane back and forth so that the flames didn't pass over him as he brought the plane down. The plane finally hit the runway, and was met with fire engines and airport personnel who doused the flames. As they were putting out the fire, Major Doolittle crawled through the fuselage, brushing the ashes from his clothes. He went over to inspect the cockpit as if nothing had happened. I was mesmerized.

In 1962, Dennis Day, that wonderful Irish tenor and comedian, was asked to perform at the Doolittle Raiders reunion. The reunion was attended by the group of fliers who flew off an aircraft carrier to bomb Tokyo. This amazing foray was memorialized in the movie *Thirty Seconds over Tokyo*, with Spencer Tracy portraying General Doolittle. Every year the pilots would convene in a different city, this year it was in Camden, Arkansas. It was held in a local motel owned by one of the Raiders.

Each year the roll call was read, and those that had died were remembered. There was a large breakfront which held the same number of glasses as there were Raiders, and for each Raider who had passed on, their glass was turned over. On the top shelf was a bottle of brandy which was carefully poured into each man's glass. They would salute their departed comrades and drain their glasses. Legend has it that the last remaining Raider would drink to all who had died. Until one day when there would be none.

It was a weekend occasion and everyone was in their civvies. You couldn't tell a PFC from a General! Dennis and I hung out with the guys all day exchanging stories. One in particular, I found very interesting, his name was "Hank." The night of the dinner and show, everyone came in their full-dress uniforms. "Hank" came strolling into the lobby in full regalia. He was literally dripping in "fruit salad," a euphemism for medals and battle ribbons. Dumbfounded, I asked, "And what are you?" "Admiral Henry Miller of the Pacific Fleet," he replied. He certainly had me fooled that afternoon in his casual attire.

We sauntered outside, where several groups of the men were standing around talking. As I stood around talking to Hank, I noticed General Doolittle in the next group. I excused myself and walked over to the General. I just had to talk to him. I brazenly tapped the General on the shoulder. He quickly turned and looked at me quizzically, I blurted out, "General, may I have a word with you?"

"Don't call me General, my name is Jimmy, call me Jimmy," he ordered.

I said, "Okay, Jimmy, can I tell you a story?"

"What kind of story?" he replied.

"A story about you, Jimmy," I answered.

He laughed and said, "I love to hear stories about me," and put his arm around my shoulders and walked away from the group to hear my story about him. I told him about watching his plane burst into flames at the Thompson Trophy Race in 1930. His mouth fell open and looking at me wide-eyed, said, "You saw that!" I told him that indeed I had, and that I stood next to his son the whole time. He was flabbergasted. From that moment on I was his buddy.

At the end of the weekend we all departed for home. Jimmy was flying to Los Angeles and I was invited to accompany him on his plane. We landed at Dallas on the way back to LA for refueling. The field was alerted that General Doolittle was on the plane. When they opened the

Al Lerner

door and we deplaned, a full military honor guard stood at attention on each side of the red carpet unfurled just for him. I will never forget that wonderful weekend. To be in the presence of that giant of a man still gives me goose bumps. He was my idol when I was a child, and he remains that to this day. He was my hero.

Marie "The Body" McDonald

In 1964, I was called and asked if I would like to accompany Marie McDonald to Australia. I was to conduct for her, and, as I was soon to learn, be her "keeper." As soon as I accepted I knew I would have to write new arrangements for her. I also had to set up rehearsals with Marie before we departed for Sydney.

Gene Mann, her manager, and I had met briefly during my years with Dick Haymes. He had been a producer at the Greek Theater in Griffith Park in Los Angeles. Gene had a good reputation in the industry, so I felt comfortable accepting the job. I was a sucker for a trip to Australia.

I went to Marie's home to help her select the songs we would use in the show, and to get her singing keys for all the tunes she would ultimately perform. This was our first meeting so I had no idea what to expect. I rang the doorbell, and after what seemed like a very long time, Marie answered the door. Without so much as a hello or go to hell, she greeted me with "I don't feel well."

After she selected a few songs that she liked, I said, "Let's get your keys and vocal range." Marie looked at me as if I had lost my mind. "I have a four-octave range, so just write them in any key," she said. It took every ounce of self-control I possessed to keep from laughing in her face. In all my years as a professional pianist and conductor, I had never heard such a stupid and outlandish statement. She really didn't know any better. I wonder if she could even sing "The Star Spangled Banner" with that amazing range! I was thinking to myself, what have I gotten myself into? A contract is a contract so I persevered. I prepared myself for a long and bumpy road ahead. We accomplished virtually nothing during our first meeting. Each time I tried to set up a rehearsal she claimed that she never felt well enough. I told her we would rehearse when we got to Australia.

In the sixties, Quantas only departed from San Francisco for Sydney. We were to meet at Los Angeles Airport for the first leg of our journey. As was my custom, my wife, Ruth, drove me to the airport and dropped me off at the curb. I took my luggage from the trunk and as I started for the terminal, I saw a group of people and police at the entrance. Marie had not been making the payments on her car and they had come to impound it. Gene Mann had taken her to the airport, so, about the time I arrived, he stepped in and said he would take over the payments. Marie was permitted to leave so she could fulfill her engagement down under.

When we got to San Francisco, we had another problem. Marie had several large bags with her and was insisting they go in the cabin. She refused to check them. The captain, who was a good friend of mine, walked over to me and said, "Al, she can't take all that stuff aboard." Marie walked over and said to him that she wasn't well and absolutely had to have all these things with her in the cabin. The captain shrugged his shoulders and motioned for one of the attendants to get her things on board. I'll never forget the look my buddy gave me. If I read him correctly, he was thinking, you poor sap! Once airborne, thankfully, she fell asleep. I finally had a little peace and quiet. I didn't have to deal with her again until our first stop.

In those days there were no nonstop flights to Australia, so we landed in Fiji, which is a duty free port. Marie wandered around while I kept my distance. I just let her do her thing, whatever that was. Quantas called our flight for departure in about an hour and everyone boarded the plane except Marie. I asked the stewardess if I could go back into the terminal and find her. There she was standing at a counter looking at watches. She wanted to buy one but didn't have any cash with her. She asked me to advance her forty bucks so she could buy the watch. I didn't know it then, but she was to cost me a lot more than the price of a watch. I paid for the damn thing and herded her back onto the airplane.

Her arrival in Sydney was very uneventful, and she was upset. She had fantasized that there would be throngs of people screaming and hoping to catch a glimpse of her. As luck would have it, Queen Elizabeth had just arrived; the press and the populace were much more interested in getting a glimpse of Her Majesty. Marie was bitterly disappointed and very upset by what she perceived as a deliberate upstaging by The Queen.

We arrived on Friday and were not opening until Monday night. This gave us ample time to rehearse. Marie went to her hotel, The Chevron Hilton. I went to my apartment near King's Cross, the Sherwood Flats, delighted to be away from her for the rest of the day.

I woke up Saturday, refreshed and ready to work. I called her hotel to no avail. I tried all day Saturday and again on Sunday. Late Sunday afternoon, I finally reached her. When I explained I had been unable to get her, without missing a beat, she stated that I must have been calling the wrong room, as she had never left the hotel. I was in no mood to argue. I let it go.

I immediately went to her hotel, she opened the door of her room with a familiar refrain, "I don't feel good." She further instructed me to take her music, rehearse the orchestra, and meet her on Monday at Chequer's, the club where she was to appear. To this point, I had never seen her music or rehearsed what I had written specially for her. I anticipated total disaster.

I walked into the club prior to our one o'clock rehearsal to try and make some sense of her music. Fortunately, I had worked with most of the musicians before, so I prepared them for a catastrophe. I took out every piece of her music that looked playable and hoped that she was familiar with them. Our rehearsal was scheduled to last from one to four o'clock. She arrived at five minutes to four. The musicians had long tired of waiting for her and had begun to pack up their instruments. They were due back at the club at seven o'clock when they would play a short dance set before the show.

I asked Marie where she had been. Instead of answering my questions, she blurted out, "I found an apartment!" Attempting to hide my anger, I shot back with, "Why didn't you find one tomorrow? We're opening tonight." Oblivious to all that was happening around her, she announced that she was going to her dressing room to start putting on her makeup and getting ready for the show. In the wake of all the chaos she was creating, she had the gall to ask Dennis Wong, the owner of Chequer's, to put larger watt bulbs in the sockets around her dressing table mirror.

The bewildered fellows in the band looked at me as if they had just witnessed a train wreck. What they didn't know was that was just about what they were going to see happen. This woman was on a collision course with disaster. They asked me what they were supposed to play; I shrugged my shoulders and said, "Your guess is as good as mine. We'll play it by ear; watch me closely."

Show time! Marie was announced and I played some entrance music. Suddenly, she appeared. I gasped audibly at what I saw walking across the stage. "The Body" was attired in Capri pants and a blouse. There was dead quiet in the room as she walked over to the mike and said to her audience, "I have to apologize for my attire, but my entire wardrobe was stolen." Australian audiences are unfailingly polite, and they sat there in stunned disbelief as did the boys in the band. It flashed back in my mind at that moment that this is the same woman who had been found wandering in the desert around Palm Springs claiming she had been kidnapped. Anything for publicity! We struggled through a couple of numbers, when she said, "I'd like to introduce my musical conductor." She turned and looked at me and, to my amazement, uttered, "What's your name?" There was a ripple of laughter in the audience. The band by now had formed an opinion of her and sat there stony-faced wondering, I suppose, when this horror of a show would be over. I really don't know how we managed to get through that night, but that's why we're called professionals. What a debacle!

Marie left the theater between shows and went to her apartment. When time came for the second show, no Marie. I realized then I would have to find her a companion to keep her going. I called an old friend, Geoff Gardiner, who had told me he thought she was very terrific looking. He was delighted to help me; little did he know what he was getting into. "Please get her to the show on time," I pleaded.

Second night, first show, no Marie. Dennis Wong wasn't a man to put up with this, and he immediately canceled her out of the rest of the engagement.

I was waiting for Marie in her dressing room when she showed up for the second show. She strode into the room like a diva; all that was missing was a pair of greyhounds. She demanded that I leave immediately so she could get ready for the show. I was furious with this behavior by now, but through gritted teeth managed to maintain some semblance of civility as I said to her, "There is no show; don't you understand it's over?" I didn't realize that the door was ajar. The chorus line had witnessed the entire scene. As I walked past the girls to leave the club, I overheard one of them say, "Poor old lady." Marie was forty-one years old.

Dennis Wong advised me prior to canning Marie that I should show up every night, dressed and ready to work for the remainder of the contacted engagement. It was common knowledge in the business that Marie had a drug problem, and that for the next twelve days we would be in Australia, I knew Geoff would look after her while I fulfilled my part of the contract.

The next day, following her dismissal from Chequer's, I called Geoff and asked him to look in on her. He went to her apartment that afternoon and was sitting in the living room talking to Marie when she picked up the phone and called the police. She said there was man in her flat stealing her jewels. Dumbfounded, Geoff, always the gentleman, waited for the police to arrive. Geoff was a very well-known man-about-town in Sydney, and the police were well acquainted with him. After questioning him and Marie, it because quite clear to them that Marie was obviously high on something. They asked her if she had a coat, she replied that she did. They asked her to get it and when she came back with it, they draped it around her shoulders and whisked her off to a mental hospital.

I showed up every night at Chequer's dressed for work because I fully intended to get paid for the entire engagement, my arrangements and the watch I had paid for in Fiji. Toward the end of the engagement, a friend of mine had a cocktail party in my honor at his apartment. My friend, Wolfie Pizem, was and is the most successful restaurateur in

119

Al Lerner

Australia. He owns three of the finest eateries in Sydney. At this party, a gentleman kept looking at me; he finally walked over and introduced himself as a reporter of one of the large Sydney papers. He had interviewed Marie a few days before we met. He went on to say to me, "I've been watching you, and you don't seem to be the kind of bloke Marie said you were." Somewhat miffed, I asked, "What kind of bloke would that be?" He told me that Marie had said to him that the reason she couldn't work was that I never showed up at the club, because I was off somewhere with some broads and that she couldn't work without her conductor. Enraged by these remarks, I looked him straight in the eye and said, "I wish you had printed what Miss McDonald had said because I would have owned the paper you work for." I turned and walked away in disgust. The next morning, I picked up a newspaper; imagine my surprise when I saw the headline: *Police Drag the Bay for the "Body."* Marie had escaped the mental institution by climbing out a window!

Marie was still in the hospital and I didn't know when they planned to release her. At the end of the two weeks, I couldn't get away from Sydney soon enough. I was thoroughly embarrassed by Marie's behavior. To soothe my jangle nerves and restore my sanity, I decided to fly up to Hong Kong for a few days. I would visit my old friend and jeweler Bing Luk and get a little rest and relaxation before going back to Los Angeles.

I arrived in Los Angeles and immediately notified the Musician's Union that I wanted to press charges against Marie McDonald for the salary due me, and my arranging fees.

A hearing was set and I show up at the union office to find Marie, her manager and attorney present in the boardroom. Their claim was that I had left her stranded in Sydney and went to Hong Kong. Because this meant she had no musical director or pianist she was unable to perform. Max Herman, President of the Musician's Union, turned to me and asked me if this was true. I said, "Yes, I did go to Hong Kong," and reached in my pocket, pulled out my canceled plane ticket and asked him to look at the departure date from Sydney. He read out loud the date on the ticket, stating that it was after the two-week period of the so-called engagement at Chequer's had ended. I won that point.

I then brought up the issue of the arrangements I had written for her. Marie claimed that they were bad, in fact, they were unplayable. I had a copy of them, and pulled them out of my briefcase, placed them in front of Max and said, "Do these look unplayable to you?" Max, always the professional, said they would have these played and make a determination. Max brought in the group of musicians, who played the arrangements from start to finish. At the end of the session, they were given a quality approval rating. Marie, her manager and attorney were notified that I was to be paid for my two-week engagement in Australia. Does it come as any great surprise to learn that I never received a dime? A few months later, I read in the *Los Angeles Times* that Marie had died of an overdose. This came as no shock to me. I witnessed her self-destruction up close and personal. What a sad ending to a life of self-destruction.

Allan "Hello Mudda" Sherman

I met and joined Allan Sherman in the sixties as his musical director and pianist. He was probably the most brilliant person I had ever known. Supposedly when he took his physical for the army, he recorded the highest IQ of any that had registered.

We went to Reno to appear at the Nugget for two weeks. One afternoon he walked over to a crap table and started playing. I watched as he put down some bets before a roll. He bet on the line behind the line and bets on the number with odds. He rolled the dice and won on most of his bets. The crap dealer stood there and paid off the bets. Allan watched as he finished paying the bets. As the dealer started to walk away, Allan said, "You've shorted me fifty cents." The casino manager was called over to review the whole sequence. After he was finished with the count, he said to Allan, "You're right," and handed him a half dollar more. He added the coin to his considerable winnings and walked away from the table.

The following Monday afternoon Allan looked at me and said, "I'd like to do an album here, "Live From The Nugget."

"When?" I asked.

He looked me straight in the eye and said, "Thursday."

"You're asking me to write all that music in four days," I said.

"Sure," he said. "You can do it, I can write all the parodies."

We started working immediately and after the second show every night I wrote 'til morning. I gave the manuscripts to a music copyist that just happened to be in the house band.

Warner Records sent their crew up on Thursday and we did it.

Al Lerner

It came out fine and is called *Allan Sherman, Live From The Nugget, Hoping You Are The Same.*

At one point in our musical relationship, we were booked into the Fairmont Hotel in San Francisco. We both enjoyed the engagement and Allan was extremely well received by every audience. After our late show on several nights we would we would go to Chinatown to eat in one of our favorite restaurants. The Chinese gentleman who owned it was very well respected among Chinese officials.

One evening while at his club, the owner asked Allan if he would speak to the Chinese people on the steps of City Hall to commemorate the Chinese New Year. Allan was honored and accepted. The following afternoon we appeared for the ceremony.

After all the introductions, the acknowledgement of the contributions of the Chinese Population in America, Allan was introduced. He began by saying, "On the Chinese calendar this is the year 3500. On the Jewish calendar this is the year 3850. Do you realize that the Jews had to do their own laundry for 350 years?" The crowd roared.

Allan Sherman, 1964

Vamp 'Til Ready

In the early seventies Allan and I wrote something to be recorded called the "Golfer's Bible." A very funny non-religious parody. We tried it out at the La Costa Country Club, where they loved it. Shortly after this date, I left to take a musical group on a cruise to Mexico. When I returned my wife, Ruth, told me about a long conversation she and Allan had had that morning. He was especially enthusiastic about the "Golfer's Bible." He was anxious to know when I would be home so we could get together and begin working on it. Unfortunately, that evening the late news reported that Allan had died. It was reported that Allan was entertaining friends at his apartment. He had ordered Chicken Delight to be delivered. While eating a piece of the chicken he choked on a bone and subsequently passed out. The guests thought he was having a heart attack, and called the paramedics. He died en route to the hospital. We had not yet heard of the Heimlich Maneuver.

I've always regretted that I wasn't with him, but I'll always remember and cherish our friendship and our wonderful and never dull working relationship and "Goodbye, Fadda."

Shani Wallis & Richard Pryor

In the mid-sixties, I toured a while with Shani Wallis, a very talented English actress and singer. In fact, she was the female lead in the stage and movie versions of *Oliver* and introduced "As Long as He Needs Me."

We played Australia a couple of times, including one of the first performances at the newly built Opera House in Sydney to raise money for the Brisbane Flood Relief.

We came back and opened at Harvey's Wagon Wheel at the South Shore of Lake Tahoe. The opening act was a rather new and fresh comic by the name of Richard Pryor. He was very clever and different. We were both booked for a two-week stint. Richard started gambling and arriving late or not at all, so we had to be ready to go on a moment's notice. At the end of the first week he was already overdrawn, so anything could happen.

At the close of the first week as he finished his act, he said, "I have a couple of friends who were across the way at Harrah's and are in the audience; it's tradition in the business that the star has the privilege of introducing guests in the audience, but screw her!" We were standing in the wings ready to go on. When Shani heard what Richard had said she ran out on stage in an absolute rage, screaming at him, "And screw you," then she began to hit him. Of course, the curtain came down, and everybody who was backstage ran out to separate Shani and Richard and quiet them down.

The production singer grabbed Pryor and shoved him away. Richard grabbed the production singer, raised his fists and growled,

Al Lerner

"Come outside, I'll kick the shit out of you." The singer calmly said as long as you know you can beat me, there's no point in fighting. The stage manager came over to me with a look of utter relief on his face and said, "Boy am I glad they didn't go outside, this singer fought Randy Turpin for the middleweight title in England."

Tony Martin

In 1967 I received a call from Al Sendry, Tony Martin's musical director. He needed a favor of me. He asked if I would fly up to Lake Tahoe and stand by to take over for him. He had to be at MGM to write music for a movie he had contracted for. He hadn't told Tony about leaving temporarily because he wanted to be sure he had covered himself with someone Tony would be happy with. Al told me he would take care of getting my accommodation and asked me to conveniently have a tuxedo with me.

I was between jobs then and decided what the hell. Tony was a very good singer and I thought it might be a nice change. I arrived and Al asked me to join him in Tony's dressing room. After he introduced me to Tony, he told him that he had to leave for a few days. Tony became very angry at hearing this and berated Al in front of me. It was very awkward and tense. Al broke in and said, "Look, Tony, Al Lerner happens to be at the Lake and offered to help me out, and I know you will work well with him." Tony was still very angry, but what else could he do? You might say Al Sendry had him over a barrel. At this point I had enough; they were talking about me and the situation as if I were the invisible man. I stood up and said, "Hold it, I am here trying to help in this situation, if you don't like it, I'll leave!"

The room because very quiet for a moment and then Tony apologized and agreed to go along with the uncomfortable situation. Al Sendry gave me the music for the show as he didn't need it. He had me sit up front so I could follow the show and music and get an idea of what would be required of me.

I anticipated no problems and went backstage after the first show to Tony's dressing room. Al and I were going over some minor aspect of the program when Tony stood up and stated, "Al will direct and play the second show!" He also told Al to stay away from backstage as I was to be in complete charge at that point.

We started the second show with a play on after Tony's introduction. We segued into the opening number and when he finished the song, as was his custom, he bantered with the audience. We began the second number, which was a ballad with Tony and the piano, alone. I began to play and Tony began to sing, when about halfway through the number Tony stopped me. I was dumbfounded, this had never happened to me before during a show. I knew I had not goofed, so I was bewildered and confused about what was going on. Tony turned to the audience and said, "This is the first time I've heard the right chords." I was so embarrassed. Even if it was a backhand compliment of sorts, it was cruel and unprofessional in my opinion. It didn't stop there; he followed up his statement with "Ladies and Gentlemen, I would like to introduce my new conductor, Al Lerner. Al, take a bow." Hesitantly I got off the piano bench, did a quick bow to the audience and quickly sat back down at the piano. I felt so bad for my friend Al Sendry. I was not prepared for what Tony said next. Al Sendry was standing behind the curtain observing all that was going on stage. Tony turned and looked in the general direction of where Al Sendry was standing and said, "Sendry, you can leave anytime." This was the beginning of my tenure with Tony Martin. Not an auspicious start.

We completed the Tahoe engagement and on closing night, Tony asked me to go to Seattle with him for an engagement at the top of one of the large Holiday Inns. By now I knew what Tony was capable of, so I told him as tactfully as I could, that he would only say something like what he said to Al Sendry to me once. He said, "Oh no, I would never say anything like that to you." I should have seen the writing on the wall.

We went to rehearsal at the Holiday Inn the evening before our opening because most of the musicians had day jobs and were not available until them. This gave me a clue as to what I could expect from them musically. They entered the show room and set up. Tony came in and said, "Everybody to the bar, let's have a friendly drink." As the musicians passed me they all said, "What a great guy."

Vamp 'Til Ready

We rehearsed for about an hour when Tony stopped and said, "Everybody to the bar." Now the musicians were really impressed, and perplexed. They had heard that Tony was a difficult guy to work with. His behavior toward them seemed to negate that rumor.

Fortunately, we had brought along a well-experienced drummer as I got vibes that something was about to happen. Call it intuition, but when you've been in the business as long as I have you get a second sense when things aren't as they seem. Then I hear the band, whoa! I didn't need intuition, it was pretty bad, I knew for sure then something was going to happen, but what?

The following night we opened to a very small crowd, which didn't help matters or Tony's attitude. After of a couple of numbers, Tony turned around and told the band to leave the stage. They all laughed that little nervous tense laugh one hears when they're not sure what's going on. They apparently thought it was a joke. They were badly mistaken! He repeated, "Off the stage." I froze! I watched sadly, as they quietly packed up their instruments and filed out. A wave of disgust washed over me as I thought this was the most disgusting moment of my career. I still had the drummer and I motioned the bass player to stay. We only did the one night, and the rest of the engagement was mutually canceled due to lack of ticket sales.

When we got to the airport, Tony handed me an economy-class ticket. I looked at it and said, "What's this?" I had always traveled first class with everyone else, so this came as a surprise and I thought it was rather insulting. He answered me with, "There has to be a captain and a private." What a joke. I walked away from him and over to the ticket counter. I asked the agent, "How much more for a first-class ticket?" She replied, "Eighteen dollars." I gave her the eighteen dollars, and went back to my seat to wait for boarding. I lagged behind for effect and when everyone had been seated in the first-class section, I boarded and entered the cabin. Tony looked at me and said, "What are you doing here?" I smirked and said, "I have a first-class ticket and I don't have to sit with you." I proceeded to take a seat as far away as I possibly could, and enjoyed the solitude. I rolled the events of the past week repeatedly in my head; I wasn't used to this behavior and had second and third thoughts about what I had gotten myself into.

The next date was at Harrah's in Reno. We had a young girl vocalist on before Tony. As she completed her show, Tony walked out and gave her a big hand and said a few clever and nice things. After a few minutes he turned around and looked at me and said, "That's your cue; don't fall asleep." I could not believe my ears and I was fuming. We finished the show and I disappeared. I was concerned about what I might say or do, so I thought it prudent to just leave and cool off.

For the rest of the date I made myself scarce; Tony only saw me as the lights dimmed and I took my place on stage. Tony tried to reach me at my hotel, but I had left word that I wasn't accepting any calls other than long distance. I finally received a call asking if I could do a theater-in-the-round tour with Ed Ames and the Count Basie Band. I jumped at the chance — no, I leaped! I phoned Tony to tell him I was leaving him. Tony asked me to come to his hotel suite as he wanted to talk with me. I said I'd be right over. We sat and I told him that I could not work with anyone who was as rude and disrespectful as he had been. He apologized and I accepted his regret over his behavior on stage.

I told him that I had accepted a tour with Ed Ames. Tony then told me that he had a tour in South Africa and he wanted me to go. He asked me if I would limit my tour and join him for the African stint. I mulled it over, I had always wanted to see Africa and now here it was. I wondered if I could put up with his behavior, but he had just told me that he would mind his manners. My lust for the lure of Africa won out over my common sense and I accepted. I arranged to leave the tour early so I could return home and go to Africa with him.

When I arrived back in Los Angeles, I called Tony to let him know I was back and ready to go. There was a long silence, and then he proceeded to tell me that he and his wife, Cyd Charisse, had started rehearsal using his old pianist Hal Bourne. They decided that Hal would go to Africa with them as long as he had been working with them in my absence.

I was livid! I had left my tour, as we had prearranged, to join Tony. He said we would get together again after Africa. I couldn't believe my ears, for him to think I would just let this breech of ethics go by the boards! No Way!

Tony asked me to phone his manager, Cal Ross, and work out a financial arrangement for my loss of the work I had just left. I laughed when Cal offered me one week's salary. I told Cal, one month's salary is what I want. Cal scoffed at this and asked me, "Are you going to sit around and do nothing for a month?" "No," I shot back, "I'm going to play tennis for a month and you're going to pay me." I slammed the phone down in complete and utter disgust.

I then went to the Musician's Union and spoke with our President, Max Herman. Max phoned Tony and asked him to have a check on his desk within forty-eight hours or he would give the story to the press.

The check arrived within the allotted time. Need I say that I never worked with Tony again? Time has a way of making all these things seem pretty irrelevant. When I run into Tony occasionally, we are cordial.

Eddie Fisher

Through the years after my tenure with the Big Bands, I had built a reputation between the agencies and personal managers. I was one of the top choices to accompany their musical stars as musical director on their personal appearance tours.

In the mid-seventies, I was called for a tour of Australia, Chicago, and Florida with Eddie Fisher. I considered it very carefully as I had heard many negative stories about his purported problem with prescription drugs.

After careful thought, I accepted, feeling that I could help Eddie get back on track. He started coming to my home every day, where we discussed every aspect of his career. He was very frank and promised that he would do anything to get back to his former status in the music scene. I told him I would do everything in my power to help him achieve this goal.

Eddie and I began to work, and one afternoon we stopped to take a break from rehearsing his show. We began chatting and Eddie told me that he had spent over two million dollars with jewelers for gifts. He also told me he had hired boxing champion Barney Ross as "gofer." A gofer is essentially a house boy, doing menial tasks, running errands and being at the beck and call of the employer. I was so depressed when I heard this; what a degrading way for such a champion and wonderful person to end up. But, "what goes around comes around." Buddy Hackett was once the opening act for Eddie Fisher, and then Eddie was the opening act for Buddy Hackett.

The day of departure finally arrived and we met at Los Angeles Airport. He was accompanied by a young woman, whom I had never met before, and a gentleman I knew only slightly. His task was to take care of Eddie and his wardrobe and so forth. During the flight I only saw him as he boarded, I noted that he was unusually quiet. I didn't see him again until we landed in Sydney.

After landing we were whisked into a room set up for the press to interview VIPs from all walks of life. Eddie was led to a table where the reporters and photographers were assembled. This was actually the first time I had seen him since leaving Los Angeles. I was stunned by what I was seeing and listening to. Since I had been to Australia so often, most of the press knew me. One of the reporters took me aside and asked me what was wrong with Eddie Fisher, as he was hardly communicative. Of course, I protected him by telling him that Eddie had been working a lot and was very tired. I think they bought my excuse.

We were then hustled off to our hotel, one of the finest in Sydney. The Westfield was owned by Frank Lowie. Frank had come to Australia years earlier as a Hungarian immigrant. He started in business with a pushcart and became one of the wealthiest men in Sydney. Mr. Lowie was also the president of the Club Haacoa where we were to perform. Eddie and his girlfriend were given a large, beautiful suite of rooms. Eddie's wardrobe man and I were given beautiful single rooms. We also had a Rolls-Royce and driver at our beck and call.

Although I had never worked with Eddied before, through the musical grapevine you hear all about the star's strong points, weaknesses, their temperament and their foibles. Eddie was likeable, with a rather boyish presence, a nice, pleasing voice and a large following. On the other side of the coin, he had very little musical knowledge, and a very limited sense of rhythm. I also had heard that on his TV. show he had his man (a pianist) kneel under the camera and mouth the words so that Eddie could stay in time.

Knowing all these musical pitfalls, I told Eddie to relax and I would go to rehearsal the next day a couple of hours ahead so I could run through the show with the band.

I came to the club and asked for quiet while I explained the problems we would probably encounter. I had worked with most of these musicians many times before on previous Australian engagements, and I knew their work and they knew how I worked. At first they looked at me with skepticism, but they trusted me and did what I asked. I told them to "stop playing" when I waved them out, and pick up when I indicated. Of course, I was at the piano all the time to follow him closely.

Eddie came to rehearsal a couple of hours later in an obvious foggy state of mind. We started his opener as he walked around the stage, which was about four feet above floor level. As he was walking around, he fell off the stage to the floor. Fortunately, he didn't hurt himself. We somehow managed to get through rehearsal. I was looking forward to our opening with fear and trepidation of what could and did happen.

We went back to the hotel and Eddie said he and his friend were going for a walk. I said it was a great idea and it would relax him before the show.

I dressed in my formal attire at the hotel. Eddie had his man handle his clothes so he could change at his dressing room at the club. I went to his dressing room to talk over a few last minute items while he was getting ready to go on stage.

He sat on a chair to put on his tuxedo pants and proceeded to fall off the chair onto the floor. I started to reach down to help him, but his man waved me off as he knew Eddie would be embarrassed.

SHOW TIME: We played him on and somehow got through the first few numbers, then we went into "If I Were a Rich Man" from *Fiddler on the Roof*. He started to sing, and the theater became eerily quiet! He started wandering around the stage without uttering a sound. I was conducting from the piano, and my conductor part had the lyrics written under the music. After what seemed like an interminable silence, I looked out into the audience and was greeted with a collective look of utter disbelief. I picked up the microphone from inside the piano and commenced to sing "If I Were a Rich Man"! Of course, the guests didn't pay to hear *me* sing. That ended the performance and the engagement.

Our itinerary after Australia was to have been Chicago and Florida, but agents and promoters have their own grapevine, which was activated immediately following this fiasco. As a result, those engagements were canceled immediately.

On the way home, we had a brief stop in Tahiti. That was the last time I saw Eddie Fisher, to this day. I'm sure he didn't see me either.

Australia
Glenn Miller

Australians are incredibly patriotic and are very caring and respectful of their veterans of every war, but most especially World War II. Aussies have a really big soft spot for Glenn Miller and his band. I got the idea to put together a group of musicians, who were with Glenn Miller, and take them to Australia. The idea was enthusiastically embraced by an Australian promoter. I assembled original members of the band who were still active. These tours included Ray McKinley, drummer, Al Klink, Zeke Zarchy, John Best and Billy May on trumpet, Willie Schwartz, clarinet and alto sax, the Modernaires with Paula Kelly, Jr., and me. I would augment with local Australian musicians to complete the Glenn Miller sound.

In 1985 we played the Queen Elizabeth Theater in Sydney. It is a very beautiful theater with a marble staircase leading up the balcony. Our group was asked to come to the theater the morning before we opened for a television newscast and interview. Simultaneously, the movie was *The Glenn Miller Story*. The television show producers asked us to come dressed in our tuxedos and bring our instruments. They staged us walking down the staircase playing "American Patrol" as we descended.

We were poised at the top of the staircase when the director yelled up to us, "Action!" We started down the staircase slowly and deliberately. We made it without incident all the way to the bottom stair, when Willie Schwartz, who was famous for his wit, blurted out, "We look like a bloody wax museum!" Everyone fell out of formation, doubled over with laughter. Too bad they didn't keep that in the newscast, it would have been a keeper.

The movie was shown and after the credits, the curtain opened to the live Glenn Miller Band playing "In the Mood." Only difference between us and what had just been seen on the screen was that we were older and grayer by forty-five years.

We went on to Melbourne for a few concerts and then we were asked to play a grand party for Prince Charles and Princess Diana. This was the highlight of this tour. The party was held in the large building on the grounds of the Melbourne Racetrack. We played throughout dinner and afterwards for dancing. During one of the numbers, I looked up from the piano and saw a young couple walking toward me. It was Charles and Diana! They came over to the piano and watched me play. I wasn't sure what the protocol was, so I finished my number. I stood up and nodded, but they immediately made me very comfortable. They asked me about the music and then, to my utter surprise, brought forth an album where I was featured on the piano and asked me to autograph it. I could have burst with pride. After all, how many people get to be in the company of royalty under such circumstances?

Coda to a Full Life

Reflecting on my life from the prelude to the coda, it has been a montage of great experiences and relationships that can never be duplicated. I've had some wonderful years with bands during the Big Band Era. Of course, you had to be young to be able to cope and withstand the hard life of doing 40 one-nighters by bus; donning your uniform in the men's room of a ballroom and shaving there with cold water. When the audience saw you on stage, it all looked so glamorous; it was our job, nothing glamorous about it.

After leaving the bands, I conducted, played and arranged music for the greatest singing stars of that era: Dick Haymes, Frank Sinatra, Perry Como, Vic Damone, Rosie Clooney, Kay Starr, Ella Fitzgerald, and many more. That was entirely different.

When my wonderful wife, Ruth, and I started our family, I limited the amount of time touring. After Ruth died in 1987, I spent most of my time home alone, deeply grieving. When I could, I visited with my two daughters, Cecilie and Ann, and my grandson, Jason. I felt like I was sleepwalking through every day.

Then, one day I visited an old friend who was now living in a specialized Alzheimer's unit. A very lovely lady came to take me to his room. On the way I found out she was the director of the unit and responsible for putting it in place. After my visit, she once again escorted me out of the unit. As we walked down the hall, I noticed a piano against the wall. I asked her if anyone ever played it, and she said no. I asked her name, she told me her name was Jonne' Arkin. I told her I would be happy to play for her patients; she thanked me for my offer. About three weeks later this nice lady called and said they were having an open house for family and friends of the patients.

Al Lerner

They would be serving cake, ice cream and coffee. I reminded her that I had offered to play for such an occasion, but that I had a fee. A little taken aback by this remark, she asked, "What is your fee?" "Cake, ice cream and coffee," I responded.

The guys of the band get together years later

She was a widow and soon we were seeing each other. She proposed to me and I had the good sense to say yes, and sixteen years ago we began our life together. We both congratulate ourselves on a regular basis on our great good luck. We have had a wonderful life together. I will always remember her words, after she told me we were getting married. She said, "You already are in love with me, so it's time to stop feeling guilty. I will never have that part of your heart that will only belong to Ruth, but there's enough room there for me too."

We still travel, play tennis, and have many good friends. We enjoy our children, Ann, Cecile, Cynthia and Spencer, and especially our grandchildren, Jason, Emma and Sophie. My wife, Jonne', is still busy as a Clinical Psychologist in private practice, and I write piano books for a big publisher, plus commercial jingles. We have been so happy, had so many adventures, and tried so many new things, that I know she has enhanced my life. I know if you asked her, she would say the same about me. What a lucky man to have had two beautiful women, both of whom loved me and whom I have loved dearly.

There are times when I can see the light at the end of the tunnel. When that happens, I change the bulb. Until then, I will just keep on Vamping 'Til Ready.

BearManor Media
PO Box 71426 • Albany, GA 31708

FOR ALL THESE BOOKS AND MORE VISIT
BEARMANORMEDIA.COM

Coming in September!

HOLD THAT JOAN
BY BEN OHMART
Finally, a biography of one of the funniest, most overlooked comediennes of the th century. The star of television's *I Married oan* and the film classics *o d That host Sho siness*, *Thin Ice* and many more, very little has been documented about oan's comical career — until now.
ISBN 1-59393-046-1
$24.95 + $3 US P&H

TALKING TO THE PIANO PLAYER
BY STUART ODERMAN
Interviews with Marlene Dietrich, Frank Capra, Colleen Moore, ackie Coogan, Madge Bellamy, Aileen ringle, Allan Dwan, Adela Rogers St. ohns, Douglas Fairbanks, r., and more!
ISBN: 1-59393-013-5
$19.95 + $3 US P&H

THE FIRESIGN THEATRE
BY FREDERICK C. WIEBEL, JR.
The only book you'll Ever need about the past/present/future masters of American satire. The utterly futile yet complete history of The Firesign Theatre and its also complete recording history is bundled together in one too-large book!
ISBN: 1-59393-043-7. $29.95 + $3 US P&H

NAMES YOU NEVER REMEMBER, WITH FACES YOU NEVER FORGET
BY JUSTIN HUMPHREYS
Illustrated with over photographs, Names interviews the unsung character men who often outshone the stars that surrounded them.
ISBN 1-59393-041-0
$19.95 + $3 US P&H

Presenting the best in nostalgia and entertainment books...
www.BearManorMedia.com
1-800-566-1251 (Order line only)

BearManor Media
PO Box 71426 • Albany, GA 31708

FOR ALL THESE BOOKS AND MORE VISIT
BEARMANORMEDIA.COM

LINGERIE FOR HOOKERS IN THE SNOW
BY WALT DISNEY SINGER ROBIE LESTER
An Audiography by Robie Lester. For 7 years she was the Disneyland Records story reader. And don't forget the singing voice for Eva Gabor in *The Aristocats*. Now you can read along and listen to this famous voice actress' musical cues in her OWN book/CD!
ISBN: 1-59393-058-5
$16.95 + $2.50 US P&H

WE BOMBED IN NEW LONDON
THE INSIDE STORY OF THE BROADWAY MUSICAL LATE NITE COMIC BY BRIAN GARI
Eddie Cantor's grandson's true story of one man's tenacious plight to get his musical mounted. From its romantic inception to its eventual demise and the score's resurrection in cabarets and recordings, this book takes you on a journey through the ups and downs of the theatrical world with all its excitement, disappointment, laughter and hope.
ISBN:1-59393-051-8
$19.95 + $2.50 US P&H

VIC & SADE
BY BILL IDELSON
Long-time cast member Bill Idelson has penned the first history of the beloved radio show, *Vic & Sade*. Complete with a prolific amount script excerpts and photos from his personal collection, this is the perfect book for all you Vic and Sadists out there!
ISBN: 1-59393-061-5
$24.95+ $3 US P&H

NOT SO DUMB
THE LIFE AND CAREER OF MARIE WILSON
BY CHARLES TRANBERG
Ready for the first biography on blonde, bubbly Marie Wilson? Was she really that vapid? Well—read the book on this *My Friend Irma* star for just $19.95 + $2.50 US postage and find out!
ISBN: 1-59393-049-6

Presenting the best in nostalgia and entertainment books...
www.BearManorMedia.com
1-800-566-1251 (Order line only)

BearManorMedia
PO BOX 71426 · ALBANY, GEORGIA 31708

ARCHIVES OF THE AIRWAVES
Roger C. Paulson's epic encyclopedia of Old Time Radio
This seven-volume set from historian Roger C. Paulson, twenty years in the making, promises to be the most complete OTR encyclopedia ever written, featuring biographies of even the most obscure series and stars. A must for any fan of radio!
$21.95 EACH. SEVEN VOLUMES

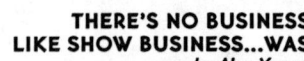

THERE'S NO BUSINESS LIKE SHOW BUSINESS...WAS
by Alan Young
You've heard Wilbur speak about *Mr. Ed* — Now read what Alan Young has to say!
$14.95 ISBN 1-59393-053-4

CORDIALLY YOURS, ANN SOTHERN
by Colin Briggs
Written by a regular contributor to *Classic Images*, this first book on Ann Sothern contains many rare pictures from the author's personal collection.
$24.95 ISBN 1-59393-060-7

FIBBER McGEE'S SCRAPBOOK
If you want to know more about Fibber McGee & Molly...
From Fibber McGee's (Jim Jordan) early years, to his final days. Includes a seven page biography of Fibber McGee and Molly and Jim Jordan, plus over 100 reproductions of original newspaper and magazine clippings and photos. Not sold in stores!
$15.00

THE RONALD REAGAN MURDER CASE
by The Firesign Theatre's David Ossman
A comedy mystery novel. Radio star George Tirebiter discovers that the apparent murder of Ronald Reagan's movie double could have been an early CIA double-cross, fabricated by Bill "Wild Bull" Casey! Could our beloved ex-President actually be his own stand-in?
$19.95 ISBN: 1-59393-071-2

HOLD THAT JOAN
THE LIFE, LAUGHS AND FILMS OF JOAN DAVIS
by Ben Ohmart
One of the funniest, most overlooked comediennes of the 20th Century. The star of television's *I Married Joan* and film classics *Hold That Ghost*, *Show Business*, *Thin Ice* and many more, very little has been documented about Joan's comical career — until now.
$24.95 ISBN 1-59393-046-1

SON OF HARPO SPEAKS
by Bill Marx
Not merely a Marx Brothers book, but an intriguing journey down an amazing highway of discovery, and love. This is Bill Marx's story.
$24.95 ISBN 1-59393-062-3

RUSS COLUMBO
THE DEFINITIVE BIOGRAPHY
by Tony Toran
The only detailed biography of Russ Columbo the man, the singer, and the enigma.
$29.95 ISBN 1-59393-055-0

ADD $2.50 POSTAGE FOR EACH BOOK

ORDER THESE BOOKS AND MORE! VISIT WWW.BEARMANORMEDIA.COM

Printed in the United States
92061LV00007B/70-195/A